The
Astral
Projection
Guidebook

The Astral Projection Guidebook

Mastering the Art of Astral Travel

ERIN PAVLINA

ISBN-13: 978-1491246979
ISBN-10: 1491246979

Book design by Maureen Cutajar
www.gopublished.com

To all the intrepid explorers
of the unknown. Be brave
and you will see all.

ACKNOWLEDGEMENTS

Thanks go out to my product manager, Stephan van Coppenole, for handling all the details so I could concentrate on writing.

To Erin Ashley Kerti for her feedback, encouragement, and support in reviewing the book to make sure I was making sense.

To Traci Shoblom, for her excellent copywriting.

To Maureen Cutajar at GoPublished.com for handling everything including the editing, design, and formatting. I'm so glad you do what you do.

And to the thousands of people who emailed me asking about astral projection…this book exists thanks to you.

CONTENTS

Part 1

Understanding Astral Projection

Chapter 1 My Astral Projection Experiences 3

Chapter 2 Astral Projection Basics 10

Part 2

Preparing to Project

Chapter 3 Preparing Your Environment 21

Chapter 4 Preparing Yourself Energetically 27

Chapter 5 Sleeping and Astral Projection 34

Part 3

Achieving Separation

Chapter 6 Indicative Sensations 49

Chapter 7 Emotional Control 55

Chapter 8 Leaving Your Body 61

Part 4

Navigating the Astral Realms

Chapter 9 Traveling 75

Chapter 10 The Planes... 87

Chapter 11 Interacting with People and the Environment................. 95

Part 5

Safe Traveling

Chapter 12 Protecting Yourself.. 113

Chapter 13 Interactions with Low Vibrational Beings.......................... 121

Chapter 14 Avoiding Astral Projection 131

Part 1
Understanding Astral Projection

CHAPTER 1

My Astral Projection Experiences

THE SCIENCE FAIR

My journey into discovering and eventually mastering the art of astral projection began, ironically, at my junior high science fair. I had decided to do my project on dreams and their interpretations. My teacher warned me it wasn't a very scientific topic, but I would not be dissuaded.

We were required to read at least three books on our subject, but when I got to my local library, I found eleven books I wanted to read on this subject. For me, it wasn't just a school project, it was a subject that fascinated me completely. I checked out and read those eleven books cover to cover.

From studying my books, I learned all about dreams, how to interpret them, and how they were tied to our sleep cycle. But in the process I also learned about two other phenomena I had never heard of before: lucid dreaming and astral projection. I was intrigued.

Lucid dreaming is when the dreamer becomes aware that he is dreaming while he is still dreaming. That sounded super awesome to me. I wanted to learn how to master lucid dreaming very badly.

The second item, astral projection, sounded like a fairytale. It was described in my books as an out of body experience, where people reported leaving their bodies and traveling on another plane, while fully aware and NOT asleep. I really didn't think such a thing was possible, but I was curious nonetheless.

I decided to start with lucid dreaming. It took me about three months of study, effort, and experimentation before I had my first lucid dream. After that, I learned how to control my dreams and even program the dream I wanted to have in advance. More on lucid dreaming later, but it was an important first step for me to eventually learn how to astral project.

Once I was well-versed in lucid dreaming, I decided to try having an out of body experience. This was not nearly as simple as learning lucid dreaming. I really had no reference experience for it, and didn't even know what I was shooting for. The books at the time were quite vague on how to achieve one, they mainly described what it felt like once it happened.

Getting to the place where I could initiate an astral experience was elusive. I tried meditating. I would lie in my bed, breathe deeply, quiet my mind, and imagine I was outside of my bedroom. Nothing. Although I could easily and vividly imagine myself somewhere else, I wasn't actually there. I was simply inside my imagination.

Then I tried mentally projecting myself to my ceiling so I could look down on my body. Nothing. Again, I could easily imagine it and visualize it, but I never escaped my body, I only escaped my mind.

I tried adjusting what time of day I tried it – before I went to sleep, upon first waking in the morning, during naps, and just spontaneous times like in math class when I was bored. Failure.

Since I had mastered lucid dreaming, I decided to try dreaming about astral projection. I reasoned that if I could just know what it felt like to fly around outside my body, then maybe my real soul could really leave my body. I had success dreaming that I was flying, but that wasn't astral projection. I couldn't even mimic projection in a dream because I hadn't experienced it in real life, so I had nothing on which to base my programming.

I tried looking for real people who had real success but found none. I read everything I could find on astral projection, which wasn't much back then in the 1980s. With no friends who had ever done this, no Internet, and getting all my information from books in a library, I was very limited in my reach.

I worked on this for three years with zero success. I was frustrated. I decided that astral projection was a fantasy and people didn't really leave their bodies consciously. I gave up on ever learning the skill. I stopped trying completely.

MY FIRST ASTRAL PROJECTION

I started tenth grade in 1984. By this point, I was fantastic at lucid dreaming but had given up on astral projection. When I started my new school, I met two people who would become my closest friends, and who would become integral in my study and mastery of astral projection.

The first was a girl I met in Spanish class, and we clicked and hit it off as friends instantly. We had the same sense of humor, and were a little bit "out there" compared to our peers. To protect her identity, let's call her Ashley. From day one, we bonded like sisters and slipped into a very easy and close friendship.

The second person I met was a boy. Let's call him Jared. I was crushing hard on Jared, and the beauty was, he was just as "out there" as Ashley and I were, maybe even more so. He was into the occult and liked studying the paranormal.

It wasn't long before the three of us would put our heads together and be discussing all manner of crazy arcane things. It was so nice to finally have people to talk to who understood me and accepted me for who I was. It allowed me to open up more to my own internal intuitive abilities, and explore unusual things without fear of judgment. I was so grateful for Ashley and Jared's presence in my life.

Some of the things we played at were telepathy, dream sharing, and a fun game where we tried to get someone to look up at us on telepathic command. Neither of them had ever astral projected, so they were also a dead end to me in terms of having an expert to learn from. That was all right though. I didn't really care at this point; I was having fun with everything else we were doing.

But everything changed on January 7, 1985. That was the night my 15-year-old self finally experienced astral projection. It was unlike anything I'd ever experienced before or could even imagine.

I went to bed like usual. In the middle of the night I woke up in my bed, on my back, and felt an intense tingling sensation throughout my entire body. It was like someone had attached electrodes to me and current was passing through my body. It wasn't painful, but it was intense and extremely unsettling.

The next thing I noticed was that I could see my room, but could also feel that my eyes were closed. I thought that was particularly unusual. How could I clearly see my room, in the dark, yet my eyes were closed?

Next I became aware of the presence of three other beings in the room with me. If I had to physically locate them, I'd say they were up near the ceiling to my left. Their presence was distinct and palpable. I didn't have much time to consider who they might be, what they wanted, or whether they were friend or foe, but their presence was unmistakable.

Next there was a high-pitched whining sound in my head. I can only describe it as the sound of acceleration. Kind of like the sound a jet airplane makes as it's speeding down a runway getting ready to take off into the sky. A fairly apt analogy as I was soon to discover.

To my absolute horror, I then started feeling my "self" being pulled slowly out of my body. It felt like someone had grabbed hold of my soul and was dragging it out of my body. It was not a comfortable sensation whatsoever. It didn't feel natural, normal or healthy in any way, shape or form.

I was so terrified that I tried to scream, only no sound came out of me, nor did I have any control over my mouth. I was trying to resist being pulled, and I felt like I was choking. Then one of the beings in the room spoke to me in my mind. It said, "Breathe through your nose, it will be easier."

So I concentrated on my nose and started breathing through it, only that had the opposite effect I was hoping it would have. I started getting pulled out much faster. I went back to trying to scream, again to no avail. But my resistance and strong desire to get back into my body where it was safe did have the effect of merging me back in with my body.

Just when I thought the experience was over, the tugging started again. Something was pulling me out of my body! I did not want to go. For what seemed liked several minutes, this tug of war was happening with "them" pulling me out and I pulling myself back in.

Finally I heard one of the beings say, "This isn't going to work. She's too frightened." Another responded with, "She's got to learn one way or another." The original voice said to me, "It's okay, just let it happen."

I responded mentally with, "Nope. Not interested. Forget I ever wanted to learn this stuff. I'm over it. Just please let me back into my body and I'll be a good girl." Eventually, I made it fully into my body and got control of it once again. As soon as I could, I sat up and turned on my light. I sat there with my knees drawn up to my chest, shaking a little from the trauma.

What does one do when one has just had their soul assaulted? There was no hotline I could think of to call. I didn't want to wake my parents. I knew they'd think I was nuts. I wasn't so sure I wasn't! I stayed awake until morning and got ready for school. I was completely haunted by the experience and preoccupied with what had happened.

When I got to school, I ran into Jared in the parking lot. He gave me a quick hug and said, "So I tried to contact you telepathically last night while you were asleep, but I guess nothing happened."

I looked at him in shock and burst into tears. I beat my fists on his chest and said, "No, no, something *did* happen." For some reason, I blamed him for my experience. I thought maybe he had opened a door that I didn't really want open and without even warning me. I was upset.

I told him about my experience, and he told me that a demon was trying to possess me. I'm going to insert right here and now that he was wrong, it was not remotely a demon trying to possess me, but at the time, and with no experience or experts in sight, I believed him, which was unfortunate because it put me in a place of deep fear.

THE ROAD TO MASTERY

The door was open. I now knew what it felt like to be separate from my body, at least a little. In the seven days that followed that initial experience, I had three or four more incidences just like it – an astral tug of war over my soul that made me ridiculously fearful of turning out my light at night. I would wake up, feel the tingling sensation, hear the high-pitched whine, and start moving out of my body. I would scream, resist, fight back, and get back in, only to be tugged out again. I must have looked like a banshee at the end of the week. I had gotten very little sleep and I probably looked like I'd been dragged through hell. That's certainly what it felt like.

Although I assumed each experience was an attack, I did notice that the three presences in my room didn't seem evil. They seemed more like patient teachers…the kind that push you out of an airplane even though you're scared to sky dive because they know you have a parachute and won't jump on your own. Spirit tough love, as it were.

I eventually realized they weren't going to give up. Jared promised he would find a way to protect me, and Ashley got me a crystal to use as a talisman. They were both as supportive as they could be, but they couldn't prevent the nighttime experiences.

After the first week, the experiences died down a bit. They happened maybe once per week. I was finally getting some sleep, and things were returning mostly to normal. Ashley and Jared were researching as much as they could, and we were trying different things to get a handle on it all.

Finally, Ashley hooked me up with a friend she met through work who was a couple of years older than us. Let's call him Sam. Sam was an experienced astral projector and someone I could talk to who wouldn't think I was nuts. I remember the first two-hour conversation we had. He really set my mind at ease.

Sam explained that the reason the experience was so terrifying was because I was afraid. Uh, damn skippy I was afraid! But Sam taught me that I didn't have to be afraid, and that the reason I was having a terror reaction was because I thought something was trying to "get me."

He taught me how to initiate the astral separation on my own, how to change my frequency so I wasn't on the "fear channel," and he explained all the ins and outs of astral travel in a way that made perfect sense for me.

Within a few months, I had made such good progress that I was able to astral project at will, protect my soul and my body while projecting, and I even learned how to go after and put down any low vibrational being that attacked me. I went from zero to hero in a few short months.

Once I got on top of the astral wave, I surfed it regularly. I loved astral projecting, exploring, experiencing, and dealing with astral bad boys. What I once had thought impossible became just as easy as lucid dreaming. By the time I'd reached my early twenties, I'd projected at least a thousand times, and had so many awesome adventures, experiences, and insights.

If it wasn't for Sam, I'm not sure what would have happened to me. My desire for everyone reading this book is to learn to astral project without fear, and know how to handle themselves on the astral plane. That is why I've written this book, to be the guide for you that I wished I'd had before it first happened to me.

Astral projection doesn't have to be frightening. If you're already experiencing projection and you're afraid, I will help you understand how to avoid those experiences. If you're new to astral projection, I'll teach you how to safely and effectively travel the astral realms and enjoy the process!

Throughout the rest of this book, I'll share more of my stories to help illustrate my points. Let's get ready to fly. Your journey is upon you!

CHAPTER 2
Astral Projection Basics

It will be helpful to understand exactly what astral projection is and what it isn't, so that as you foray into this realm you'll know what to expect and what it's really all about. This chapter will cover the basics and answer some common questions people have about astral projection, which will help you decide if this is something you even want to commit to learning.

WHAT IS ASTRAL PROJECTION?

Let's start with a basic definition. Astral projection refers to your soul, spirit, or consciousness leaving your body. Astral travel refers to your soul moving around outside your body on the astral plane, or other planes of existence.

Is there a difference between the terms *out of body experience* and *astral projection*? Functionally, no. They both refer to the soul leaving the body. But in practical terms, I would define out of body experiences as those happening spontaneously to people who had no intent of leaving their bodies, and I would classify astral projection as those who consciously and with intent decide to leave their bodies. In this book, we'll be discussing astral projection.

CAN ANYONE LEARN TO ASTRAL PROJECT?

I believe it's possible for anyone to learn how to astral project. The same way it's possible for anyone to learn a sport. Success at that sport depends on how much effort you put into learning it. Just as some people are more naturally gifted when it comes to sports, with astral projection I do find there are certain factors that make it easier to learn.

You've got the time. Learning astral projection will take time. You'll need to study, practice, experiment, interact with experts, learn new skills, and more. But if it's very important to you, just set aside some time each day or each week to make progress. This is a practice that builds success over time, so if you put in the time, you'll be much more likely to achieve it. But you can't go to bed every night wishing and hoping it will spontaneously happen to you.

You're patient. It's unlikely you will master astral projection right away. There will be starts and stops. There will be sudden or spontaneous small successes followed by weeks with no progress. There will be "almost got it!" moments followed by intense feelings of frustration about why it's taking so long. Or you might get lucky and it all just comes together for you in a weekend. There's no way to predict. But at this point you've got to be ready for this to take a while, and you've got to be ready to be patient.

You're willing to experiment. I spent three years experimenting and even though in that time I had no real success leaving my body, I was priming myself for success later. I mastered lucid dreaming; I mastered meditation. I learned how to research. And I learned lots and lots of different ways how *not* to do it. All of that happened because I was willing to try, willing to experiment, and willing to fail until I succeeded.

You're young. When it comes to astral projection, it appears that young people, between the ages of 13 and 18, have a natural advantage. I suspect this age group has an easier time learning this because they have not yet been taught it's impossible, they are not saddled with a lot of responsibilities such as paying bills, managing relationships, or worrying about their health, and paranormal activities tend to be strong at these ages.

However, that doesn't mean that older people can't learn it. Older people sometimes have a harder time believing it's possible, and they're more fully rooted in the material world than kids. But age has its advantages. Likely, older people have more self-discipline, are better at studying and learning, and can spend a little money to interact with experts, take classes, or buy support items like meditation programs.

You're open-minded. If you decide in advance that this is impossible, you will surely fail, unless you have a spontaneous out of body experience or a near-death experience to wake you up. But if you believe this is possible and if you keep an open mind about it, you will allow it to happen and attract the experience more easily.

You have a strong desire. Nothing takes the place of conscious desire. If you truly wish to learn how to astral project, you can. Follow the map that others have laid out before you, and you will get to the top of this mountain. It may be difficult, it may be frustrating, it may take a long time, but you can make it, one step at a time. Desire and will power are what will keep you going when frustration sets in.

DO WE ASTRAL PROJECT IN OUR SLEEP?

There's a lot of discussion and opinions on this subject. Some spiritual teachers will tell you that every night when you go to sleep, your soul leaves its body and travels on the astral plane, and you can wake with no memory of this. Some believe dreams come from the astral plane, and you go there every night to have them. I don't agree with this philosophy at all.

When you leave your body, you remember it. You can't help but remember it because your entire consciousness leaves your body behind like a peanut leaving a shell. If you don't remember the experience of leaving your body, you didn't leave your body. Astral projection is a 100 percent conscious experience.

When you dream, you may not remember what you dreamed because you were unconscious at the time. But when you astral project, trust me, you'll remember it. You'll feel more conscious than you do right now. It's a ridiculously high-awareness experience that will feel more real to you than being in your body.

So no…you don't astral project every time you sleep. Your astral body may become "active" but not leave your body. To use our peanut analogy, it's like shaking the shell and hearing the peanut rattling around. Rattling the shell doesn't mean the peanut has escaped the shell. It just means the peanut is separate from the shell but still contained within it. More on this when we talk about sleep, dreams, and astral projection.

IS ASTRAL PROJECTION SAFE? CAN YOU DIE?

This is a question I'm asked frequently and with good reason. Astral projection can be very safe, or it can be very unsafe. It's like asking if skydiving is safe. With a functional parachute and knowledge on how to use it, skydiving is very safe. With no parachute, it's very unsafe. Why do beekeepers wear those white protection suits? Because they know they're going to interact with a hive full of bees, and they don't want to get stung.

With the right awareness, education, and equipment, astral projection is extremely safe and extremely rewarding. But with no training, with the wrong mental state, or interacting with the wrong entities, astral projection can become a thrill ride into a nightmare that can leave you bruised, battered, beaten, and worn.

It can damage your mind, it can deplete you of vital physical energy, and it can cause psychological damage. Sometimes people have encounters that leave them with low physical energy. Sometimes people develop anxiety, hallucinations, psychotic tendencies, and even thoughts of suicide. Sometimes people attract low vibrational entities that attach themselves and drain mental, physical, and psychic energy. It's not something you want to go into blind.

On the other hand, there is nothing more exhilarating or wonderful than astral projection. It leaves you with a sense of completely knowing that you have a soul, that the soul can survive outside the body, and that there is life after death. For many, that certainty is worth all the risk.

But can you die? Truthfully, how would we know if anyone died during astral projection? They wouldn't be able to come back to tell us. I personally believe it's possible to die during an astral projection, but I also believe the probability is very low. Your astral cord keeps you tethered to your body (more on that later) and there are guardians out there who protect you while you project (more on them later too) and it would be extremely unlikely that you die. But you've been warned. So learn to do it safely and you should be just fine.

There is a risk in any activity. Walking out of your house can kill you. Skydiving can kill you. Having a baby can kill you. Make peace with the fact that death is possible, and protect yourself as best you can.

CAN ASTRAL PROJECTION BE PROVEN?

There are studies that have been conducted to prove whether astral projection is real. They usually involve putting a random object someplace where the subject can't see it, then asking the subject to project, fly to the location, and then report on what they see. It's a good experiment. But when subjects are successfully able to report on the object, some skeptics say, "It doesn't prove they projected, it just proves they're telepathic, or could read someone's mind, or are able to do remote viewing." Hey, that's not bad either!

But I understand why people want proof. The most reliable way to prove astral projection is real is to learn to do it yourself. I'm not sure we have an iron-clad reliable tool that can measure astral projection. If you need proof in order to attempt it, you may be waiting a long time. My recommendation is to do it yourself and see how you feel.

One of the best proofs I've had in my own life happened one night while I was in my teens and still living at home. I woke up inside my body, sensed some evil presence in my home and decided to go investigate it. I lifted up out of my body, flew down the hall and down my L-shaped stairs. Just as I turned the corner, I saw my father walking up the stairs. With no time to stop, I flew right through him. I took note of the time when I got back to my body, and the next morning my dad reported hearing strange flapping sounds in the house. He got up to investigate and went downstairs. He was coming up the stairs at the exact time I flew through him.

This is not irrefutable proof, nor am I claiming it is. But when you can report on things other people are doing, and you had no idea they were doing them, that's fairly good evidence, at least for yourself.

One day, science will catch up and develop tools we can use to test our theories. In the meantime, if you want to play scientist, go study science. If you want to astral project, learn how to do it and experiment yourself or with friends.

One great experiment is for one person to randomly select a card from a deck of cards, and place it on their night table by their bed, face side up. Then have your buddy who is a master astral traveler fly to your house and look at the card and report back to you the next day. Keep a log of your efforts and see what you find.

WHO SHOULDN'T ASTRAL PROJECT?

Although I believe astral projection can be safely enjoyed by anyone, there are some conditions under which I feel a person should think long and hard before attempting to learn this skill.

People on certain medications. If you are on any medication that causes drowsiness, suppressed breathing, or hallucinations, you should not astral project while you are on those drugs. During astral projection, you may encounter situations that require you to get back into your body quickly, turn on a light, or stay very alert. If your body drags you back down into a sleep state, you are vulnerable to attack.

People with sleep apnea. Sleep apnea is a condition where you stop breathing for short periods of time while you're sleeping. It can cause you to wake up gasping for air, often with no memory that this is occurring. If you have a sleep apnea episode and you are not in your body at the time, you are risking a serious health situation. Without your soul in your body, your body doesn't move. With sleep apnea, you may need to turn over onto your side to help you breathe, and most of the time that people project they do it from their backs. So be careful if you're prone to apnea episodes.

People looking for an escape or distraction. A lot of people who gravitate towards astral travel are looking for more than their own lives can provide. Whether that's excitement, danger, or adventure, you can become addicted to astral projection and spend too much time playing in the astral world. Please use astral projection responsibly. Your body needs you in it. And your life is worth living. Don't use astral projection to avoid handling the things in your life that you need to handle. They'll just be waiting for you when you get back anyway.

People who want to spy on others or be bad guys. Yes, when you're astral you can see what your friends are doing, you can spy on the president of the United States, and you can watch girls taking showers. But come on now. Have some moral fiber. If you wouldn't do it while in your body, why do it outside of your body? Plus, you're going to find that when you're astral, those banal human things aren't of interest to your soul. It's not going to be as easy to accomplish as you think it will.

The other concern is that if you sink to a depth where you violate the freedom and privacy of others, you're moving to a vibration that could easily attract some of the more negative entities that wander the astral plane. Do you really want them to be your new best buddy? Attached to you? Whispering things in your ear when you're not able to slough them off? You've been warned.

People who aren't committed to safety. Astral projection can be an amazing spiritual experience. Or it can become a nightmare. If you jump into the shark-infested ocean without a cage to protect you, you're asking to get bitten. It's like climbing a rock face with no rope or safety harness. Yeah, you *might* make it, but with the right equipment you can do this safely. Invest in the time and knowledge to make this a safe experience for yourself.

Suicidal or depressed people. Astral projection will put you right in the middle of being alive and dead. If you're suicidal, you could probably find a way to cut your astral cord and be done with life. If you're depressed, you may be tempted to stay out of your body a lot longer than is healthy for it. It's like scuba diving with a sinus infection, or trying to climb a mountain with two broken legs. Your best astral experiences will come if you are whole in body, mind, and spirit. Otherwise, you're going to be a tasty morsel to a stronger entity who wants to eat you for breakfast. Please project responsibly.

Part 2
Preparing to Project

CHAPTER 3

Preparing Your Environment

Now that you've decided you want to learn astral projection, let's get into the nitty gritty of learning how to do it. Before you step one toe outside your body, you need to prepare yourself for what lies beyond. Otherwise, it's like jumping over a cliff and hoping there's a big body of water below you instead of really hard ground.

In the next three chapters, you'll learn how to prepare your environment to support your endeavors, how to prepare yourself energetically to increase your odds of succeeding, and you'll learn how sleep, dreams, and mastering your consciousness can help you learn how to project at will.

SELECT A LOCATION

Let's start with something basic. Where do you think you'll be projecting from most often? Probably not your desk at work or school. Probably not your car while you're driving. You'll need a nice, safe, controlled environment where you can safely store your body while your consciousness roams the universe. If your body doesn't think it's safe, it will resist you leaving it.

The three most common locations are your bed, your couch, or in a chair. There are pros and cons to each of these locations.

Your bed. Your bed is a great choice for several reasons. First, your body will be very comfortable and not cramped. Second, a lot of people project right before they go to sleep or as they wake up, so being in bed just means more chances to take advantage of good conditions. Plus you won't have to worry about your body falling out of position.

There are a couple of disadvantages to projecting from your bed, however. If you are attempting to project before you go to sleep, you may be so conditioned to sleep while in bed that you fall asleep before you can achieve separation. Also, if you have a partner in bed with you, they can easily disrupt your concentration, or cause your body to become uncomfortable which will cause your body to recall your spirit before you're done playing.

Your couch. A lot of people choose to project from their living room couch. One advantage to using a couch is that you can "program" it to be your astral projection location of choice, which you can use as a psychological anchor that says to your body, "Every time I lie on this couch, I'm going to project." If you get good at it, you can lie down on the couch and begin projecting immediately.

Another advantage is that you will be alone on the couch so your body won't be disturbed by your partner rolling over, stealing your covers, or kicking you under the sheets.

A possible problem with couch projecting is that you need to make sure your couch is very comfortable. If you've got hard pillows or edges sticking into your back, it could make you too aware of your body, which will block projection.

You also need to make sure your couch is wide enough so your arms or legs don't flop off. Try your couch to see if you can lie on it comfortably like you can in your bed. Tucking a blanket around you can often keep your limbs from slipping off the couch.

Another variable you'll have to control is whether your living room is a source of foot traffic. If you're taking an afternoon journey and people are walking around in the house, or watching television, or otherwise making noise, you'll be unable to get away.

Your chair. Believe it or not, you can project while sitting up in a chair. Your body does not have to be prone for projection to occur. One of the benefits of projecting from a chair is that you are way less likely to fall asleep if you're sitting up.

Another advantage is that you're definitely going to be alone in your chair, so you don't have to worry about anyone moving around in your chair and disturbing you like you would if you were in bed.

However, as you can probably guess, there are some serious disadvantages to projecting from a chair. It's much easier for your body to fall over, which will pull your astral self back into your body just in time to hit the ground. Also, your head can flop forward at the neck, leaving you with a possible breathing problem that will wake you or potentially cause you to be deprived of oxygen.

If you want to project from a chair, I recommend using a recliner where you can adjust the degree at which you are lying down. A 45-degree angle is great, but experiment to find what's comfortable for you. Being in a recliner can also act as an anchor, just like your couch. And, like a bed, you are less likely to roll out of it like you might on a couch.

Whether you use a bed, a couch, or a chair, the bottom line is to find something comfortable for your body so it's not disturbed when you leave it. If your body is in need, your spirit will come back to tend to it.

Get a Log Book

You're about to explore a vast new realm and other planes of existence. You're going to want to keep track of what you're experiencing and how you succeeded or failed so you can improve your process.

A log book doesn't have to be fancy. You basically need a place where you can write down your experiences and notes. Get a journal, a spiral-bound notebook, use a word processor, a typewriter, or scraps of sticky notes. All that matters is that you have a place to log your experiences. So acquire something and commit to keeping it at your main astral location.

When you have an experience, take note of all of the following and keep it for your records so you can use it as your own personal resource in improving your ability.

Write down the date and time. Was this at night or during the day? Was it a weekend or a weeknight? Was it within an hour of going to bed or right as you were waking up in the morning? The reason you want to note all of this is to look for patterns later which you can then use to increase your chances of success.

Log the precursory conditions or events. Did you meditate and it happened? Were you just coming out of a lucid dream when separation occurred? Did you pass out from drinking heavily? Had you just listened to some music? Write down enough information so that if you wanted to repeat the conditions, you could.

Note what happened. Then write a detailed account of the experience. Did it take you a minute to separate or was it instant? Did you fly around your house or just hover over your body? Did you see anyone or anything interesting on the journey?

Also take note of what you heard, what you saw, and what you felt. Was there tingling? Did you hear the high-pitched whine? Did you hear voices? Did you feel like someone was climbing on the bed with you? Did you see other entities?

How did you return to your body? Write down how you ended up back in your body. Did you consciously step back in? Were you snapped back? Were you blocked by a negative entity? Did a guide put you back?

Again, noting patterns will be integral to success. If you always snap back into your body due to a disturbance in your physical environment, you'll want to take steps to ensure that you'll be alone and that your environment is more controlled. If you always seem to project after listening to certain music, you can use that as your trigger more often.

You won't have to keep a log book forever. And once you're more skilled, you can just jot down some notes like this:

April 14, 10:00 p.m., meditated. Projected within 30 minutes of going to sleep. Visited my friend, Rob. Got pulled back after 10 minutes because someone flushed the toilet in the house.

Control the Environment

Nothing kills your projection attempts faster than something in your physical environment that disturbs or prevents your success. Here are some tips to control your environment so you have the best chance of achieving separation, and so you can stay out much longer.

Make sure your alarm is off. How awful would it be if you finally got out of your body, you were exploring Mount Everest, and your alarm clock goes off? Your body is going to startle, which will snap your astral body back into place. Make sure the alarm is off and that you have time to finish an experience. If this means only attempting projection on your days off when you can afford to stay in bed longer, then so be it.

Control your house sounds. Is there a grandfather clock in your house that chimes or gongs loudly on the hour or half hour? Disable it unless you're extremely good at ignoring it. Is your air conditioner particularly loud when it goes on? Use a fan instead (good for white noise too!). Do your windows rattle when there is the slightest wind? Seal them better. Give yourself every possible chance. Anything that would normally wake up your body from sleep could end your astral experience.

Prepare your pets. If you're used to sleeping with Rover on your bed, you may run into some difficulties getting out of your body. First, if Rover pounces your body, you'll snap back. Also, Rover or Fluffy may react to entities that are drawn to you astrally. I highly suggest keeping pets outside of your projection place, and make sure the door is secure. Also check the doggy door and make sure it doesn't clang or flap too loudly when the dog goes out.

People can be problems too. Does your mom wake you up every morning to get ready for school? She could interrupt a seriously awesome projection. Does your wife like to cuddle in the middle of the night? Just the act of her touching you can disrupt your astral energy and cause a snap back. Does your neighbor go to work at 3:00 a.m. and gun his engine on his way out of the driveway? You'll have to learn when to project and when it's likely to be interrupted. Does your kid get up before you do and turn on every light in the house on his way downstairs? Make sure your door is closed, your blinds are shut, and do the best you can to make sure other people's habits aren't affecting you.

If you live in a house full of people, it can be difficult to create the right environment to support your astral training. Do the best you can to set up the conditions that will lead to your success, even if that means sleeping in the guest room a night or two a week, or letting the kids have more sleepovers at their friends' houses.

CHAPTER 4

Preparing Yourself Energetically

Now that your physical location is selected and controlled, you've got to work on your energy. After all, astral projection is an energetic experience. You're going to slip onto another plane of existence, you're going to encounter other conscious beings, you're going to be challenged to keep your vibration high. Mastering your energy will allow you to achieve separation, travel safely, and handle the entities you may encounter on your journey. You'll need focus and commitment as well. If you want to learn to astral project, you can't just dabble, or it will take years for you to achieve separation.

So in this chapter we'll discuss ways to clear your mind, boost your energy, get focused, committed, and find social support.

CLEARING YOUR MIND

Your mind is running 24/7. It never shuts off. You're thinking about your responsibilities, your plans, the people in your life. You've got stress, challenges, and hurdles. At night when you're sleeping, your subconscious mind begins to process your stressors, which is why you sometimes dream about them. Or you may lie awake at night unable to sleep because you're overwhelmed or anxious about the problems you'll have to face in the morning.

When you're overwhelmed, stressed, or anxious about life's physical, material, real-world challenges, your mind will be preoccupied, which will energetically tether you to this world and to your body. It's much harder for your spirit to leave your body if you're bogged down with life problems. The mind will act as an anchor, keeping your energy focused on the physical, and prevent you from releasing your body so you can astral travel.

This doesn't mean you have to remove every stressor from your life. That would be extremely difficult, if not impossible. It just means you have to learn to switch it off temporarily so you can achieve separation.

There are several ways to get your mind clear. First, you can use meditation, which we'll discuss in depth in a moment.

Second, solve some of your problems. Seriously. Make a list of your biggest problems and see if you can get some of them off your list. Got money problems? Pay down your debt, increase your income, or get on a payment plan you can live with. Got relationship issues? Communicate with your partner, clear the air, don't ruminate or have conversations in your mind when your partner isn't even present. Failing school? Get a tutor, catch up on assignments, meet with your counselors, raise your grades. Whatever your life problems are, see if you can make some progress on dealing with them so they don't take over your mind's resources.

Third, change your beliefs. Sometimes problems and stressors can be relieved by changing your perspective about them. "I'll never get out of debt," can become, "If I continue to put two hundred dollars a month towards my debts, I'll be out of debt in 24 months." Find ways of looking at your problems that make them non-problems. Instead of thinking, "Man, I've got problems," start thinking, "I've got a situation, and these are my options for dealing with the situation." Get on top of your thinking, don't let it steam roll you into a cycle of fear and worry. Your chances of successful astral projection are greater when your mind is relaxed.

You don't have to solve your problems; you just have to learn how to put them aside so your mind can be at ease. When you go to sleep at night, you should breathe a sigh of contentment, not anxiety.

Mastering Meditation

If you can learn to master meditation, you will greatly increase your chances of being able to astral project. Meditation will help you clear your mind, release negative thoughts, boost your energy, raise your vibration, breathe deeply, and allow separation to occur. If you are not familiar with meditation, I'm going to give you a crash course right now, but you should also read up on it and practice, practice, practice!

Meditation is about breathing, relaxing, and letting go. I'll take you through the process right now and explain the components and how they relate to astral projection as we go.

Prepare your environment. Make sure the room temperature is comfortable for you. Use a light blanket if it's chilly, but not something so heavy that it makes you hot. Turn off the phone and any other distractions. Make sure the pets won't be able to pounce you. As I mentioned earlier, getting control of your environment will increase your chances of successful projection, and it's the same with meditation.

Get comfortable. Find a comfortable position for your body. I highly recommend selecting the location and position you'll be using when you project. So go to your bed, couch, or recliner and get comfortable. This will help anchor you and psychologically tie your meditation location with your projection location.

Breathing. Now that your environment is secure and you're physically comfortable, begin to do some deep breathing. Take a breath in through your nose and release it slowly from your mouth. Alternatively, you can breathe in and out through your nose. The goal is to find a comfortable way of breathing, so pick what is most comfortable for you. You want to put your body's breathing on auto pilot, but you first want to establish a deep rhythm. You also don't want your breathing to become a source of distraction for you, so find the breathing pattern you like best.

Relax your body. As you continue breathing, put your awareness on your feet and toes. Let them relax with each breath you take. Then move to your lower legs, breathe deeply, and feel the muscles in your calves relax. Move up to your knees and thighs. Continue to breathe deeply throughout the relaxation process as you relax the muscles in your body.

Then slowly move your awareness to each body part – your pelvis, stomach, back, chest, shoulders, neck, arms, hands, and finally your head. This can take just a few minutes, or you can spend 20 minutes or longer to relax your body. There are no hard and fast rules. Go at your own pace.

You may feel floaty. After you've physically relaxed your body, you may feel like you're floating or like you can't feel your body anymore. That's great. That's not astral projection or separation, but it's a good start because it means you are conscious but cannot feel your body. That will come in handy later. The goal here is for you to remain conscious without being too attached to your bodily sensations.

You may feel tingly. Some people report tingling sensations in their heads or face area. It should feel pleasant, not prickly. If you feel a tingling sensation, this is good. It's not an indication of separation but, like feeling floaty, it's good to start getting used to the sensation because it means your vibration is higher than it was before you started, and that's integral to separating easily from your body.

Thoughts. Once you achieve this relaxation, just try to be in the present moment. Don't allow thoughts about your problems or stressors to invade your relaxed state. This may take some practice. Just enjoy the sensations of floating and tingling. If you're not floating or tingling, just enjoy the sensation of relaxation for as long as possible. You are training your body to stay relaxed while your mind stays active.

Wander. Try to stay in this state for as long as you can. You may even notice you have no sense of time. Then let your mind wander. Imagine you're flying over the mountains. Imagine you're relaxing on a sunny beach with a cool breeze. Imagine you're floating in water or on a cloud. Just put your thoughts and attention on feeling relaxed and at peace. The longer you can master this sensation, the better.

Meditation will train your mind and body for astral projection. When you're ready to project, your body must feel safe and relaxed so that your consciousness can roam free. Meditation is great exercise for experiencing this.

Make a regular practice of meditating. Pick a time of day where you do it regularly. It won't hurt to meditate before you go to sleep because it will send you into your dream state in a much higher vibration, which will be helpful.

Try not to meditate sitting straight up and cross-legged. That's fine if you're just meditating for peace of mind, but for astral projection practice, get yourself into the same position you'll be in later when you project. More on positions in the next chapter.

The bottom line on meditation is to become comfortable breathing regularly, staying in the present moment, relaxing the body, and freeing your mind.

COMMITMENT AND IMMERSION

Preparing yourself to be an accomplished astral traveler is going to involve commitment and immersion. You're not going to achieve it by thinking about it occasionally, or by dabbling. How does NASA launch a rocket into space? Do they generate small bursts of power, a little bit at a time, days apart? Or do they fire that baby up and give it all they've got in order to overcome the gravitational pull of Earth? Once the rocket escapes our atmosphere, they can throttle back on the power and let it coast through space on minimal power, but to get it launched they've got to ignite a lot of fuel.

Astral projection is similar. It's very difficult to break orbit, so you've got to give it all you've got in the beginning, and then you can coast later. This means you've got to commit to studying and practicing astral projection, and you've got to immerse yourself in it completely. Every shot you take will bring you closer to achieving it, so don't let too much time pass in-between attempts, and make sure you're using every tool and trick at your disposal to make it happen.

So let's talk about ways to really immerse yourself in this study and stay committed.

Don't get discouraged. I worked at this for three years and I got discouraged. That didn't help me one bit. Go into this understanding that success is not guaranteed. You can't just flip a switch and be out of your body. It's going to take time and patience. But you significantly increase your chances of success if you practice regularly. Even a failed attempt is important. Don't quit. The time is going to pass anyway, so you may as well work on this.

Give it some thought. Go to bed every night thinking about astral projection. Imagine what it will feel like. Think about where you'll go and what you'll do. If you end up having a spontaneous experience, you'll be less likely to freak out and snap back to your body if you've got a plan for success.

Read about it. Reading books or articles online will help you immerse yourself. There are many techniques and stories out there. You never know which one will resonate with you. Don't just stick to one resource or method. Fill your mind with knowledge and pull from as many experts as you can.

THE IMPORTANCE OF SOCIAL SUPPORT

You will succeed faster at learning how to astral project if you've got a good social support system in place. I worked on astral projection alone for three years. It wasn't until I connected with new friends who were into this sort of thing that my experiences began to happen. If it hadn't been for Jared and Ashley, I probably would have stopped trying to learn astral projection. Social support will help reinforce concepts and give you someone to talk to.

Some tips on getting social support for this endeavor include:

Online forums. Thanks to the Internet, you can now connect with people all over the world who are accomplished astral travelers. Find a forum, connect online, share stories and experiences, ask questions, and learn new techniques. Just make sure that the people you're connecting with have actually done it, and make sure they're giving you advice that's coming from a positive, high vibration place.

Meet-up groups. Find a group in your area that meets regularly to practice or discuss astral projection. It's helpful to share knowledge and information, techniques and methods, plus you can meditate together. If you can't find a group that already meets, create one of your own and invite people to attend meetings.

Avoid negative people. Like any intrepid explorer of the unknown, there will be people around you who are skeptics. Avoid talking about astral projection with people who don't believe in it, or who think you're nuts. It's going to discourage you. If they're not an expert on the topic, why would you even listen to them? Trust yourself and your own experiences, and seek advice from those ahead of you on the path. They'll be able to guide you and help you navigate through the masses of information out there on this topic.

Practice clearing your mind, learn how to meditate and how to relax your body, and make a firm commitment to learning astral projection. All of these will increase your chances of successfully projecting. Stack the deck in your favor.

CHAPTER 5

Sleeping and Astral Projection

Understanding the relationship between sleep, dreams, and astral projection is going to be crucial to your success as an astral traveler. Most astral travelers hit the astral trail right before they go to sleep, right as they are coming out of sleep, or in the middle of the night when they are between dreams. You must understand the role that sleep plays in astral projection because you'll use it to your best advantage in helping you slip out of your body.

In this chapter, I'll explain how body position and time of day affect your success. I'll also cover lucid dreaming and how it relates to astral projection. And then we'll talk about how to master your consciousness.

BODY POSITIONS

Does it really matter what position you're in when you astral project? If you're leaving the body behind, why not just leave it in whatever position it happens to be in? Body position does matter. Here's the deal...unless your body "agrees" to the separation, then separation will not happen. You might think your soul is in charge, but while you are incarnated, your body has control of the ship, and you must coax the body into letting you out for a joyride in the cosmos.

The body has a primal instinct and need to keep your soul in your body. That's what keeps your body alive and well. If the body isn't on board with you astral traveling, you won't get very far.

You're living a physical existence. Your spirit is housed in your body and acts like the battery that keeps the machine running. When you die, your soul leaves the body behind forever and the connection is severed. When you astral project, you are leaving the body, but you are still attached to it with a cord that continues to pump energy into your body to keep it functioning. But the body gets "nervous" when you leave it because it's afraid you aren't coming back. So we've got to keep the body happy so we can take trips outside every once in a while.

Anything that adversely affects your body is going to cause you to snap back to your body. If the body is uncomfortable or feels like it's in danger, you will not succeed in your attempts to leave it. So let's talk about ways to keep the body happy, calm, and still.

Body position. The best position for astral projection by far is to lie on your back. In this manner, all your limbs are resting comfortably, nothing is crossed or kinked, and your circulation is at its best. Arms at your side is better than arms crossed over your stomach or chest.

Most people project upwards, and if you are lying on your back, it is very natural to float up and out of your body, totally energetically intact, without strange positioning in your astral body. Once you get extremely proficient at astral projection, you can project from any position and be able to sort yourself out once you're astral. But for beginners, you'll want to be on your back.

If you try to project from your side, your body is more likely to get uncomfortable. Side sleepers know that you can't lie on one side for too long without having to flip over. Your hips get sore, your arms can get crunched, and your top leg lies on your bottom leg. If you decide to project from your side, you'd better have just gotten into that position, otherwise your body is going to start to feel uncomfortable and will pull you back so you can turn over.

Forget about projecting while lying on your stomach. It's confusing because most people float upward. If you're on your stomach though, you're going to either project down into your bed (which is not comfortable especially for beginners) or you're going to have to project out of your back or your head, which is more difficult and doesn't feel natural. I'm not saying you can't project from the stomach position, but it's vastly harder, and sometimes you end up lowering your vibration as you sink or plummet down into the earth. When in doubt, always go upwards.

If you're projecting from your recliner, you'll be on your back even if you're at a 45-degree angle, so no worries about that.

Bodily needs. Take care of your bodily needs before you project. If your body finds itself in discomfort, it either won't let you out or it will snap you back if you're already out. Nothing ruins a good projection faster than a full and urgent bladder.

Likewise, if you have allergies and your nose is stuffed up, try to clear that before you go to sleep. Same with a cold, flu, or other ailment that affects your breathing.

If you suffer from sleep apnea, you're going to have to take extra care to make sure your body is in a position where your breathing will continue normally. For safety, you may have to project while lying on your side.

If you're sick, have a sore throat, a stomach bug, or a migraine, you'll have a difficult time achieving separation. The only exception to this is when you have a fever, which can sometimes make it easier to project. However, I don't recommend projecting with a fever if you can help it because you're more prone to hallucinations, and you're more likely to attract negative entities. More on that in a future chapter.

Clothing considerations. What do you wear when you're sleeping? You want your body to be unfettered. If you wear a nightgown and it's all twisted, that's going to cause your body some discomfort. If you're wearing flannel pajamas, you may get too hot. If you're sleeping naked or just in your underwear, that's probably the best, but if that's not a good option for you, then wear pajamas that don't pull and tug at your body when you move around at night.

TIME OF DAY

Technically, you can astral project at any time of the day. There's no magical time that makes astral projection easier. However, each time of day comes with its own advantages and disadvantages, which I will cover in this section. In the end, you'll need to experiment with different times of day to find what's easiest for you and what gives you the best experience.

Right before you go to sleep. The advantage to attempting astral projection right before you go to sleep is that your body is at its most tired. If the goal is to put the body down so your soul is free to roam, this is a good time to make the attempt.

Use meditation to calm and relax your physical body while keeping your mind awake. You'll also be able to use your conscious will and intent to invite the sensations into your body that are indicative of astral separation.

Another advantage is that you're less likely to be disturbed. You probably just emptied your bladder, your alarm clock isn't about to go off, and you've got all night to explore without having to worry about getting up in time for work or school.

One difficulty of projecting right before sleep is that you're more likely to fall right to sleep instead of projecting. This is exactly because you are the most tired at the beginning of the night. Your brain wants the rest. Your body wants the rest. Unless you're skilled at keeping your mind awake while your body goes to sleep, this will be a difficult time to attempt it.

A way to combat this is to lie down about 30 minutes before you would normally go to sleep, before you're dead tired, so that you have time to meditate and get out of your body before it falls asleep.

Before your first REM cycle. Your sleep cycle is roughly 90 minutes long. You'll go through various sleep stages (alpha, delta, theta waves) and then you'll start to dream during the REM portion of sleep (REM stands for rapid eye movements). Then the cycle repeats. You're coming up and going down through brainwave stages all night long.

As the night progresses, however, you'll spend less time in alpha, delta, and theta waves and more time in REM. By morning, your dreams are longer, and your time in the other stages is shorter.

Projecting before your first REM cycle is an easy time to initiate a projection. You haven't begun dreaming yet, so you don't need to wake up from a dream first, and you won't confuse your experience with a dream. You can go right into separation. It's the perfect time to wake up your mind while your body is caught in the beginning throes of muscle paralysis.

The only downside to projecting at this time of night is that sometimes you're going to encounter negative entities. When you project before REM there is a tendency to be a little confused at first, which could give the advantage to the bad guy. So you'll want to project at this time of night only when you're prepared for defense and know how to switch channels. More on how to do that in upcoming chapters.

In the middle of the night. The middle of the night is a great time to project because your body is fully relaxed from having been asleep for a while, and you still have plenty of time for a nice long travel before you have to get up to start your day.

As you're moving through the various sleep stages, there will come a natural break in the middle of the night where you will begin to wake up before heading back down to sleep. This is a great time to flop yourself onto your back if you aren't there already, and initiate the astral separation.

One possible downside is that, by the middle of the night, you may need to get up to use the bathroom, which could easily wake you up so fully that you have to start the process of meditating yourself down again when you get back to your bed. If that's you, don't worry. Just get up, handle your business as fast as you can and with minimal alertness, and settle back into your bed quickly. You may miss an opportunity or you might actually enhance it. It depends on how practiced and skilled you are. If you can hold it though, it's best not to get out of bed. Just go right into a projection.

Upon waking in the morning. Many people project just as they are waking up from a full night of sleep. Often you will experience sleep paralysis at this time which is a precursor to projecting. We'll discuss sleep paralysis in an upcoming chapter, but for now all you need to know is that this is a common and ideal time to initiate separation.

The disadvantage is that you may not have much time to enjoy your journey if you have to get up for work or school. Also, your alarm clock may ring which is going to snap you back, and people in your house might be getting ready to stir and make noise. Plus, if you didn't have to empty your bladder in the middle of the night, you'll surely need to by morning.

Midday naps. One of the best times to practice astral projection is during the midday when you take a nap. Your sleep cycle is a little different during naps. You're more likely to have a spontaneous sleep paralysis episode which will give you a great opportunity to project. I'd say a third of my astral projections happened during naps. I used to come home from school and take a two-hour nap just so I could practice astral projection.

You'll want to secure your location though, and control for environmental noise and people moving around your house. Also if light bothers you, definitely nap in a darkened room. It's very helpful to nap only when you feel sleepy though. If you try to force a nap when you're not tired, you'll just be frustrated, but once you are an accomplished projector, you'll be able to park yourself and slip out of your body fast.

Planned sleep breaks. This is possibly the best way for beginners to induce sleep paralysis, which will lead to astral projection. Here's how it works. Go to sleep at your usual time, but set an alarm to wake you three hours before you normally get up. When the alarm goes off, go use the restroom if you need to, then get back into bed. Keep the lights off, don't engage in conversation with anyone, and don't start thinking about your day. Stay awake in your bed for 30 minutes and then go back to sleep. Lucid dreams or sleep paralysis are extremely likely to happen under these circumstances, and you will be able to initiate astral separation at that time.

Alternatively, when your alarm goes off, sit up in bed and turn on a dim light. Read a magazine or book, but don't get out of bed, do chores around the house, or start typing emails. Stay awake for one to two hours, then go back to sleep. Same thing will happen – lucid dream and/or sleep paralysis. Experiment to determine whether staying up for a short amount of time or a longer amount of time leads to a better outcome for you. But this is the best way to trigger the right conditions.

LUCID DREAMS

Lucid dreaming simply means you become aware that you're dreaming while you are still dreaming. There's nothing more fun than becoming aware that you're dreaming and then doing things in your dream that you can't or don't do in real life. Imagine the possibilities. You can fly, have super powers, spend quality time with celebrities or fictional characters, put yourself in an action thriller movie scenario, visit with deceased loved ones that you miss. If you can imagine it, you can do it in a lucid dream.

Lucid dreaming is the perfect accompaniment to astral projection. When you project, your mind is awake while your body stays paralyzed. In lucid dreaming, your mind is awake while your body stays asleep. Learning the skill of maintaining your consciousness while your body and brain are asleep is vital in order to achieve astral projection. So lucid dreaming becomes a fantastic and safe training ground to prepare you for the complexities, excitement, and possible danger when you project.

Learning how to lucid dream is a little easier, in my opinion, than learning how to astral project, so if you can master lucid dreaming, you'll use that skill and that awareness to help you with astral projection. It will be beyond the scope of this book to go into depth on how to lucid dream, but there are many resources and books on the Internet, and you can read my articles on my blog (www.erinpavlina.com/blog).

For now, I'll explain the difference between dreams and astral projection, how to control your emotions and excitement, how to direct your will, how to create and manifest what you desire, and how to use your consciousness to protect yourself.

Difference between dreams and astral projection. As I mentioned in the beginning of this book, many people think that we astral project every time we sleep or dream. Not so. Dreams and astral projection are totally different phenomena. It's crucial that you understand the differences so you'll know if you're having success projecting or if you're just an accomplished lucid dreamer.

When you're dreaming, you are asleep. When you astral project, **you wake up first**, and then leave your body. This is an important distinction.

When you dream, the dream was just a dream, it didn't really happen. For example, "Oh, I dreamed I was at the top of a volcano and when I looked inside, I saw kittens." That didn't really happen, did it? When you astral project, the experience is real. You actually left your body, you traveled around your house or the cosmos and could report on real circumstances. For example, "I flew into my child's bedroom and saw her stuffed dog had fallen onto the floor, right on top of her lollipop. Boy that's going to be a sticky mess." And you can go into your child's room the next day and find the stuffed dog on top of the lollipop.

In dreams, your location is just magically possible. Examples: your old room when you were a child, the set of your favorite TV show, in bed with Brad Pitt. When you astral project, you begin the experience where your physical body is located, so that will be your bedroom, the couch, or a chair. You don't project **from** Brad Pitt's bedroom, you project **to** it. There's a difference.

In dreams, you are not always conscious of who you are or what's real, and the nonsensical makes sense. In a dream, it may make perfect sense that Brad Pitt is buying you dinner. In real life, it probably isn't as likely. In a dream it might make perfect sense that you are a character in your favorite TV show, but in reality that can't happen. Alternatively, when you astral project, you are entirely conscious of the situation, circumstances, and environment. You remember who you are, that you are lying in your bed, that you are projecting. You're extremely conscious and everything is real.

In a dream, the characters you encounter are not real. They are constructed from your own thoughts and your own mind. They are part of your mental construct. In an astral projection, any beings you encounter are conscious, free, and not part of your subconscious mind at all.

In a lucid dream, you can control the actions of your dream character because you are the boss, the creator of the dream. In an astral projection, you can't control anyone you meet because they are not part of your mind, dream, or subconscious. This is why you need to know how to handle yourself accordingly.

In a dream, when the dream is over, you wake up. You realize you've been dreaming or at least sleeping. You sometimes forget your dreams. In astral projection, when the experience is over, you merge back into your body, consciously, and open your eyes. You remember what you just did and what you just experienced.

Dreaming you are projecting. One confusing situation is when you dream that you are leaving your body. It's quite possible to dream that you're astral projecting, but dreaming it isn't achieving it. If you dream you're projecting, you're still inside your mental construct, you're still just dreaming.

One way to tell it's just a dream is if you don't wake up first. Example: "I was dreaming that I was in my high school math class and all of a sudden I realized I was dreaming, so I told the dream to go screw itself and started flying up out of the ceiling. Then I was flying all over the world, and I saw my friends, and I went to the White House, it was so cool. Then I woke up." Not astral projection. Just a dream. How can you tell? You didn't wake up first in your bed. **Dreams of flying are not astral projection.**

Obtaining emotional control. In order to astral project successfully, you're going to need to learn to keep your emotions in check. Becoming too excited or thrilled with your accomplishment is going to snap you back into your body and end the experience. That doesn't mean you can't be happy that you're projecting, but if you want to stay out of your body for more than a few seconds, you're going to have to be chill about it.

Lucid dreaming, like I said, is a training ground, and it's a perfect place for you to learn emotional control. When you realize you're dreaming, nothing will wake you faster than getting too excited about it. Excitement, fear, any overwhelming emotion will trigger something in your physical brain, which will anchor you back to your body, and you'll wake up. Just like during a nightmare, don't you often wake up just as the bad guy is going to stab you with the knife? Or just before you hit the ground while falling?

Practice staying calm when you have a lucid dream, and if you can master that, your lucid dreams will last much longer, and this skill will carry right over to astral projection. When you find yourself lucid in a dream or during projection just carry this attitude, "Cool, here we go, I've got this," instead of, "Oh my god, I can't believe this is happening, I'm totally freaked out right now, and what's that creature I see coming towards my bed!" Keep calm and carry on.

Learn to direct your will. Whether you're lucid dreaming or astral projecting, you must take command of the situation. You must exert your will on the situation, otherwise you're going to be at the whim and mercy of other beings.

During a lucid dream, once you become aware that you're dreaming, you become the dream's architect. You can change the scene, you can add characters, delete characters, you can make characters do whatever you want. But you have to decide what to create. Practice doing this and master it.

If you can learn how to exert your will, then when you astral project, instead of just floating aimlessly around your bedroom or staying stuck on the ceiling, you can move with purpose and speed to your destination. Maybe you want to visit a friend. Maybe you want to go read the card that your friend has placed on his nightstand so you can prove astral projection. Maybe you want to reach a higher plane and talk to a deceased loved one.

If you know in advance what you're going to do, you'll be ready to do it when you go astral. Along the way, you'll potentially have to fight off a lower vibrational entity, and you'll want to have a solid plan for that ahead of time. More on that soon.

Learn to create what you need. In a lucid dream, if you need a sword, you just have to will that sword into existence and there it is. In dreams you can snap your fingers and create what you want; a person, place, or thing. You can change your environment, you can teleport to a new location.

The same is true during astral projection, except instead of creating it from dream material, you'll be creating what you need from the ether. We'll talk more about the kinds of things you'll need in a future chapter, but for now it's important to practice creating, so do it in your lucid dreams. Practice creating objects with a thought or snap of the fingers. When you're astral, you can't *hope* the object will appear, you need to *know* it's going to appear. Your will determines your success. If you don't think you can make a sword, guess what? No sword will be forthcoming. So practice in your dreams where it's safe, and practice so you know what it feels like to create something out of nothing.

MASTERING YOUR CONSCIOUSNESS

Even if you decide not to learn lucid dreaming, you'll still need to become aware of your consciousness in order to astral project. You can't separate your consciousness from your body if you don't know what your consciousness feels like. Lucid dreaming is the perfect place to become aware of your awareness, so I do highly recommend taking the time to learn it. Many people spontaneously learn to lucid dream while attempting to learn astral projection, so it may just happen for you, be on the lookout.

One way of beginning to master your consciousness outside of the dreamscape is during the day. Suddenly say to yourself, "Oh gosh, I'm awake, and I'm walking, and I'm about to go into that grocery store." Seriously. "But I know I'm awake of course." Do you? Prove it. Several times during your day, **consciously** acknowledge that you are an awake and aware human being.

You'll start to notice that when you're not consciously acknowledging your existence, that you'll feel more asleep, more at the mercy of the tides of life. And when you start to consciously note events happening during your day, you'll start to feel more conscious and alert more often. This is a good thing.

Another way to practice your consciousness-raising is to pinch yourself sometimes. Ask yourself, "Am I dreaming or awake?" and then pinch yourself. Do that enough during your day and you'll start to do it at night when you're sleeping, which will trigger more lucid dreams, and more chances to play in your dreamscape.

And lastly, before you go to sleep each night, say out loud or to yourself, "I will remember my dreams. I will stay conscious tonight as I sleep." It begins to program your mind.

Here is a technique I used with great success when I was learning lucid dreaming. It allowed me to remain conscious until the last possible moment before falling asleep, and I found that I had more lucid dreams because of it.

Lie on your back and stare at the ceiling. Normally when you go to sleep, you lie down, close your eyes, and eventually drift off, right? Well now you are going to keep your eyes open. Let yourself blink normally when you need to, but then go right back to staring at the ceiling with your eyes open.

You'll begin to notice that your eyelids become heavy and want to close. Every time you notice your eyelids closing, open them. Don't fling them open or force them open, just open them nice and easy. After a short while they'll close on their own again and probably stay closed longer. If you are still conscious, open them again. Keep doing this for as long as you can, until finally your eyes will close and you slip away into sleep.

The beauty of this exercise is that it will train you to stay consciously conscious, if that makes sense. You are mastering your consciousness, and only slipping into sleep when you can't hang on any longer. Try it a few times and see what it does for you. When I used this technique, not only was I more likely to have a lucid dream, I was more likely to project within 45 minutes of getting into bed, before REM sleep kicked in.

Part 3
Achieving Separation

CHAPTER 6
Indicative Sensations

You're done with preparation so let's get you out of your body! If you've done everything from *Part 2: Preparing to Project*, you'll have really stacked the deck in your favor. You'll have your log book and will have written down and noticed patterns. You'll have picked a nice location and position from which to project. You'll have controlled your environment. You'll have learned how to meditate, breathe, and relax your body fully. You'll be so immersed in astral projection that you have friends to talk to who share your interest, and you'll be thinking about it a lot before you go to sleep. You'll be dabbling in lucid dreaming or be an expert dream architect by now. And you'll have become conscious of your consciousness.

Even if you haven't mastered all of this yet, you may still begin having experiences that are indicative of astral projection. In this chapter, I'll explain the five sensations you'll get which will indicate to you that you are primed and ready to project. In Chapter 7 I'll explain how to get emotional control when you're projecting, which is crucial if you want your travels to last longer than a few seconds. In Chapter 8, I'll teach you how to get free of your body once separation has occurred.

SLEEP PARALYSIS

Sleep paralysis refers to the condition where you are awake but can't move your body at all. Your body is paralyzed, but you are fully conscious. Normally when we are conscious, we can move our bodies, right? But during sleep paralysis you will be unable to move a muscle, and yet you'll be completely awake.

This can be a very disconcerting sensation because it's literally going to feel like you woke up paralyzed. It can cause great panic and with good reason. Being unable to move your limbs is frightening. Unfortunately, fear is the worst possible thing you can allow yourself to feel while in this state, because it's going to invite a host of negative entities to you who will want to feed on your fear like you were waving a bloody limb at a shark.

In the next chapter we'll discuss overcoming your fear, but for now I want you to know that if you are trying to learn to astral project and you find yourself in a state of sleep paralysis, you should throw yourself a party, because you're right on the verge of successful projection.

Sleep paralysis is the exact state you want to be in if you want to astral project. Body asleep, mind awake. So how does this even happen? During sleep, your body secretes a chemical to paralyze your body, so you don't physically act out your dreams. Sleep paralysis occurs when you are rising up from a sleep state and the chemical hasn't worn off yet, thus you are awake but your body is still asleep. This happens most often in the morning or during naps, which is why those times are good for beginning astral travelers.

What most people don't realize is that when you are in a state of sleep paralysis, your astral body is activated. It's like the shell on the peanut was opened and the peanut is just sitting in the shell, unaware that it is free to move about the world without the shell. I've received hundreds of emails from people who describe getting to the sleep paralysis state but not knowing what to do next. I'll cover this in detail in Chapter 8.

Is there a way to activate or consciously create sleep paralysis? I haven't found a way to consciously induce it, however, there are several conditions which almost always lead to sleep paralysis. One is being on your back. Another is coming out of a lucid dream. And the third is taking a nap or going back to sleep in the middle of the night after you've been up for a short while.

For now what I want you to know is that sleep paralysis is a natural precursor to astral projection, don't be afraid of it, and get excited and happy if you achieve it.

DUAL VISION

The next indicator that your astral body is ready for separation is dual vision. Simply put, this is when you can see but your eyes are closed. Yeah, how cool is that?

When you achieve sleep paralysis, you may not be able to move your limbs, but you'll be surprised to discover that you can somehow see even though you know your eyes are closed. It's an unusual sensation. You can look all around your room and see everything you'd be able to see if your eyes were open.

The first time this happened to me, it caused me a great deal of confusion and surprise. I could clearly feel my body lying on my bed. I could clearly feel that my eyes were closed. And yet I could see perfectly, in the dark even! How is it possible to receive visual information if your eyes aren't open to perceive it?

The answer is because you are not using your eyeballs or your brain. You're using your astral vision, which I will discuss in more detail when we talk about navigating the astral realms. This astral vision continues when you are outside of your body, completely unattached to your body.

If you think it's weird, realize that when you dream, you are seeing your dream even though your eyes are closed. Vision is happening in your brain. During astral projection, vision is happening without your brain processing the stimuli.

So if you ever wake up in your bed, are paralyzed, but can still see, you are golden! Get ready.

Hypnagogic Hallucinations

During sleep paralysis it's extremely common to hear and see things around you that "aren't there." I put that in quotes because the scientists will tell you that you're hallucinating, creating these sights and sounds in your own mind. I find it interesting that most people experience the same hallucinations during sleep paralysis. Did we all get together one day and decide our hallucinations were going to match up? I don't think so, that's a pretty big stretch.

The truth is that what scientists think are hallucinations are actually other beings on the astral plane who are technically around you all the time, but which you can't see, hear or detect until you're on the same frequency with them. Think of it like coming into phase with them. You're tuning to their station, and you are suddenly able to hear and see them. In reality, they are occupying that space all the time, just on a different plane, so you don't normally interact with them. But when you astral project, you **will** interact with them. I'm here to teach you how to avoid them, deal with them, or shut them up if they're bothering you. I'll cover this in great detail in Chapter 13.

When I had my first astral projection, if you recall from Chapter 1, I heard voices explaining to me how to relax and breathe so I could escape my body faster. Those weren't just voices; they belonged to conscious beings who were trying to guide me out of my body.

In the beginning of my astral experiences, I would go from a lucid dream straight into sleep paralysis. Then the hypnagogic hallucinations would begin. I'd feel someone climb onto my bed. I'd hear the sound of doors slamming nearby, sometimes windows breaking. I'd see entities hovering over me or worse, touching my body! I'd see swarms of tiny creatures flitting by. I would hear entire conversations around me. I'd see strange lights all over my room.

If you look up "night hag" on the Internet, you will read stories of a grisly female entity who sits on your chest while you are paralyzed and is trying to choke you or suffocate you. If we're all hallucinating, why do so many different cultures report the same kind of entities doing the same kinds of things under this condition?

As I mastered astral projection and learned how to change my frequency, I was able to experience sleep paralysis without being visited by scary creatures and sounds. When you first start out, there is a primal fear, which attracts these entities to you. Once you get control of it all, then when you wake up paralyzed, you will see and hear guides, angels, and other high-vibrational beings.

My purpose in even mentioning the night hag and other lower vibrational beings is so you won't be surprised if that's what you attract. Many people write to me asking how to prevent sleep paralysis because they don't know how to handle the lower vibrational entities. Instead, I want to teach you how to deal with them instead of running scared, so that if you want to astral project, you won't turn around just as the door opens for you.

Think of them like bees. If you know the hive is there, you don't poke it. You avoid it. But if you get stung, it's not the end of the world. I don't want you to fear being in the meadow of astral projection because you're afraid of the astral bees.

TINGLING IN THE BODY

Once you are in a state of sleep paralysis, you may begin to feel a tingling sensation spread through your entire body. This isn't because you've lost circulation. This tingling sensation is your astral body "waking up" and becoming active. Tingling is your clue that your astral body is separating from your physical body. You're raising your vibration and putting your consciousness into your astral body.

When I first felt the tingling sensation, it was uncomfortable, mainly because it was odd and unexpected. It feels like an intense energy growing inside your body, and at first you have no idea what it's about so you try to resist it. It can be frightening. It almost feels like you're being electrocuted, which would be a serious cause for concern, but what's actually happening is your energetic body is firing up. It feels like your molecules are speeding up. It feels like pushing the accelerator while your car is still in park.

There's also a sensation of needing to move away from the tingling before it gets so intense that you can't take it anymore. I credit the tingling sensation with actually driving me out of my body upon occasion. It's like being struck by lightning, but it's not painful, just intense. And you feel so full of energy that you must release it or be overwhelmed by it.

As I became very skilled at astral projection, I was able to induce the tingling sensation at will. I would wake up paralyzed, think "awesome!" and induce the tingling sensation. I couldn't have induced it in the beginning because I didn't know how and had no reference experiences to draw from, but once you've had the sensation a few dozen times, it becomes a simple matter to induce it in your body. You're simply raising your vibration. You're sucking in the energy around you to help you break out of your body.

If you find yourself with the tingle, get excited. You're filling your astral gas tank and are almost ready to peel away from the curb.

HIGH-PITCHED WHINE

The fifth sensation indicative of astral projection is the high-pitched whine or buzzing sound that you'll hear when you're in sleep paralysis. I can only describe it as the sound of acceleration. If you've ever been on an airplane when it's about to take off, you know that as it picks up speed there is a high-pitched sound you hear as the pilot accelerates the plane in order to achieve lift-off.

The high-pitched whine often accompanies the tingling sensation. It's the sound you hear when you are raising your vibration to the point where you are in your astral body instead of your physical one. If you hear it, don't be scared by the sound. It can be intense, just like the tingling. But it's part and parcel to exiting your body. So when you hear it, be glad.

Just like with the tingling sensation, this sound of acceleration can push you out of your body. It's like the peanut becomes so excited in the shell that it starts vibrating or shaking, and squeals with delight as it leaps out of the shell, ready to explore on its own.

CHAPTER 7
Emotional Control

When you awaken in a state of sleep paralysis, can see with your eyes closed, start hearing and seeing things you wish you weren't, feel the tingling sensation, and hear the high-pitched whine, you have separated from your body. But you're still sitting in it.

The emails I get the most are of this variety, "I woke up in my body, heard the whine, felt the tingle, heard the voices, but nothing happened. I didn't go anywhere. Eventually the paralysis stopped, and I was able to move again. Where did I go wrong?"

You never got up and out of your body. You fired up your rockets but never left the launch pad. I'm going to teach you how to get out of your body, but first I need to explain how to have emotional control, or your rocket will launch and drop right back down to the ground.

OVERCOMING FEAR

Fear will turn astral projection from a pleasant, spiritual, exciting adventure into a hellish experience that can make you afraid to go to sleep at night. The faster you can learn to overcome your fear, the sooner you'll be enjoying the benefits of astral travel. I'm not saying you're definitely going to feel fear, but in case you do, I want you to know how to handle it and get over it fast.

So why does astral projection even cause fear? There are several reasons. First, when you wake up in sleep paralysis mode, it causes panic. You're conscious but can't move. Because that's not a usual situation for you, it may cause intense fear. You wonder if and when you'll ever be able to move again.

Second, when you begin to separate from your body, it's like a bright light going on in the dark, and entities are attracted to the light and come to investigate it. Having low vibration entities sniffing at you, tugging at you, and even sucking on your energy is also quite terrifying. It's like walking into a room and suddenly being swarmed by a thousand bees. How much worse that you can't move to swat them away?

Third, when you actually leave your body, you may see and hear things you wish you didn't. I'm not going to lie, there are some scary, nightmarish beings wandering the astral plane, and sometimes they attack you. If you're not ready and you don't know how to escape or protect yourself, you'll be very afraid.

So how do you get over the fear so you can safely project and have a pleasant experience? Here's what you need to know.

Expect the fear. Knowing that fear might happen is half the battle. Usually when someone wakes up in a state of sleep paralysis, they panic and in their minds are screaming, "Help! I can't move. Oh my god, what's that sound? Is there someone on the bed with me? Hello? Help!"

But not you. You're reading this guide book so when sleep paralysis happens to you, you're going to be thinking, "Wait, what's this now? I can't move but I feel wide awake? Oh wow, this is it. This is awesome. Hey, who are you hovering over me? Be gone foul creature, I have work to do!"

If you rail against the fear, it will take hold of you and you'll sink into the fear vibration which will make you an easy target and a tasty snack.

Similarly, when you achieve projection and you're traveling around, if you encounter a being that doesn't have your best interests at heart, you'll know exactly what to do because you'll have read Chapters 12 and 13, and you'll be a rock star!

So when you feel the fear, you'll acknowledge it and wave it away because you'll have a plan and tactics to deal with anything that bothers you, so you won't need to be afraid of anything.

Be ready. Another way to overcome the fear is to prepare yourself for what you're going to encounter. The best defense is a good offense. By the time you're done reading this book, you'll know how to avoid or defend against any entity you might encounter, and you'll know how to actively protect yourself so you can't be harmed. The more time, practice and effort you put into your preparations, the more pleasant your astral experiences are going to be.

Take a short trip. More than likely, your first astral experience will be very short. You might get a limb out of your body, or maybe you'll even make it to your ceiling. This is a good way to open the door and get a peek at the astral realms without running headlong into trouble. Don't feel you have to go too far from your body initially. Some short flights around your house are a good way to reassure your body that you aren't abandoning it. This will allow you to take longer trips later.

You're the boss. One of the biggest fears people have is the fear that something or someone can come and steal their body while they're out. This cannot happen. Your astral cord is like a bookmark or placeholder. Nothing gets into your body while you are traveling outside of it. You may encounter beings that want to attack your body, or scare you into thinking they will take possession of it, but that's not going to happen. Knowing that you are the boss of your own body should help to ease your fear.

When I first started astral projecting, I always encountered the negative entities. I lived in absolute fear of lying down at night because invariably a tug of war over my soul would begin. I was often at the mercy of the creatures that attacked me during sleep paralysis. At first, I didn't know how to fend them off, and I certainly didn't feel safe leaving my body while they were around, but eventually, with the help of my friend Sam, I learned how to protect myself, raise my vibration, and safely leave my body.

Remember that some fear is very normal, and you may get lucky and not feel an ounce of fear when you astral project. Once you lose the fear of projection, the real fun begins!

Controlling Excitement

When you get to the place where fear is no longer your master, then the excitement of being able to astral project starts to come into play. If you're not careful though, that excitement will be the very thing that prevents you from achieving projection, or snaps you back into your body before you're done playing.

When I finally learned to overcome my fears, I would leave my body and start flying around my house, intent upon visiting my family. Once that became easy, I ventured out to visit friends in other homes. I remember one time I got to my friend's house, flew into her bedroom, saw her lying on her bed and instantly became so excited to be there, to have achieved that milestone, that I got snapped back to my body. It was frustrating.

This excitement really became a problem. If I got too excited during sleep paralysis, I'd wake up. If I got too excited during a projection, I'd snap back. I was sort of annoyed at this because it had taken me months to overcome my fears, so why shouldn't I be excited about being free?

But I soon learned that excitement was just as much a hindrance to astral projection as fear. And I had to learn to stay calm and in control during every projection, or it would end much earlier than I wanted it to.

One of the most important skills you'll need to master is mental and emotional control. Without them, you'll either succumb to the low vibrational entities or you'll be taking very short trips.

Imagine the control a person in a shark cage must have, submerged in water, with scuba gear, inside a metal cage, while a swarm of sharks come towards you. If you panic, you can't breathe, or you drown. With astral projection, it's very similar. Control is everything.

So how do you stay calm in the face of something so thrilling, terrifying, and exciting?

Avoid adrenaline spikes. Nothing will put you back inside your body faster than adrenaline. Is it even possible to feel adrenaline while you're outside your physical body? I'm not sure of the physiology of it, but if you encounter a situation that would normally cause a fight or flight response, an energetic adrenaline surge happens. If you're too excited, you'll snap back. If you're super afraid, you'll snap back too. So if you want to stay out longer, avoid adrenaline.

This means not getting overly excited even when something great happens. I recall one experience where Jared drew a picture on a white board in his room and told me to come look at it so I could describe it when I got to school the next day. I had just gotten into his room and saw the white board when I became so excited that I snapped back.

Control your breathing. If your breathing becomes rapid due to fear or anxiety, you'll be unable to project. Learn to take your meditative breathing with you into all your astral experiences. When you wake up in sleep paralysis mode, try to take some deep breaths. Attempting to scream will cause your heart rate to rise, which will keep you in place.

Be an observer. One of the best ways I found to stay calm, control my fear, and control my excitement, was to project in passive observer mode. To get free of your body, you'll need to be nonchalant about the whole experience. "Yawn, just another day in astral land. No biggie. I'm just going to fly about a little and see what's going on at my friend's house. It's cool. No worries. Yeah I see you following me, you varmint, but I'm not worried. Toddle off now."

If instead, you leave your body thinking, "Oh. My. God. This is the bomb! I can't believe this is happening. I've got to hurry before something attacks me! Holy cow, what's that over there? Is that a skeleton? Holy f—!" you're going to snap right back to your body, because your fear or excitement will trigger your body to recall you to the flight deck.

Try to take the experience in stride. Try to be passive in your thoughts. That doesn't mean you can't enjoy the experience. Far from it. You'll enjoy it more if you can stay calm, which will allow you to stay out longer, and have richer experiences and interactions.

Avoid emotional attachment to the outcome. Another way to increase your success and your time outside your body is to try not to have any emotional attachment to the outcome. If you're extremely stressed, or you feel like you're in a hurry, or that this one experience is your only chance, you'll end up putting so much stress on yourself that you snap back.

You will have many chances to project. Even if you only get up and stand next to your bed looking down at your body before you snap back, you've succeeded. The next trip could be longer. Even if you only get down the street but don't make it to your friend's house, it's nothing to be concerned about. Once you become proficient at astral projection, you'll stay out longer, accomplish more, and interact with many beings. If you allow yourself to become too attached, you may give up in frustration right before things were going to get great!

In summary, the secret to getting out of your body and staying out for long periods of time is emotional control. Without it, it's like pouring water on the hot coals in your barbecue just when you're ready to grill your steak. Don't extinguish your fire, and don't stoke it either. Just be calm, cool, and collected. Be a pro. You got this.

CHAPTER 8

Leaving Your Body

The big moment has arrived. You've achieved sleep paralysis, your body is tingling, you hear the buzzing high-pitched sound of acceleration. You can see even though your eyes are closed, you're sensing, seeing, and hearing other beings around you. Your astral body is activated. You're in the rocket, and you want to take off. How do you get out of your body?

The biggest mistake people make is right at this moment. They're waiting for something to happen. They're waiting to float out of their body or start flying. They're expecting movement to just begin. But that's not how it works. Astral projection is not something that happens **to** you. You've got to happen to it. You've got to move. You've got to get up, fly up, move up, stand up, roll out, step out, stretch out…in other words, take action. Astral projection is voluntary. You need to make all the moves here. So let's discuss how to get you out of your body.

STRETCHING OUT

The most common method of leaving the body is stretching up and out of it very slowly. When you're in a state of sleep paralysis, if you try to lift your physical arm, it will not move, but your astral arm will. With your dual vision, you'll probably even see an energetic arm lift up out of your body. If you don't see it, you'll definitely feel it. It will feel exactly the same as if you lifted your physical arm.

Next, lift your other arm. You'll see it or feel it coming up and out of your body. You may also at this time feel a stronger tingling sensation. It feels like something is magnetically trying to pull your astral arms back into your physical arms. Don't let them fall back in.

If you can manage it, stretch your arms further out and let them lift the rest of your body out. Imagine you're reaching for something above you. Let your body follow your arms. Again, you're going to feel strong sensations that are going to make you want to just fall back in. Don't succumb to the pull. Keep going. It doesn't hurt to send reassuring thoughts of calmness to your body. "Shh, there there, it's all right, I'm not leaving you for good, just want to step out for a minute and get some air. There's a good body, just stay here, and I'll be right back." Stay calm and in control.

One big mistake people make in this state is trying to imagine their astral body leaving their physical one. That takes you inward, into a mental construct much like lucid dreaming. In fact, if you're not careful, you'll simply slip into a dream state and dream you are projecting or flying around.

If you actually succeed in stretching out of your body, it will feel like you are physically stretching out of your body. Because your body is paralyzed and cannot move, when you attempt to move, you're going to move your astral body instead of your physical one. This is why being in a state of sleep paralysis is the bomb diggity of all states. It will anchor your body so your astral body can get up and out.

You literally just want to stand up or sit up. Use your "muscles" to pull you to a sitting or standing position. I can't stress this enough. It will feel like you physically stood up out of bed, except, when you look down, you'll be very surprised to see your body still lying on your bed. That's because your consciousness is now in your astral body, not your physical one. In fact, you won't feel your physical body anymore at all, and couldn't move its real physical arm if you tried because you're not in it anymore.

Once you are out, you are all in! All in your astral vehicle that is! You are then free to move and travel. We'll discuss navigating and traveling the astral realms in the next chapter.

The stretching out method is the simplest and most common method of getting out of the body, but it's not actually the one that creates the most success. Read on for other ways to break your body's gravitational pull.

ROLLING OUT

Stretching out of your body happens very slowly, giving your body many chances to convince you not to leave. Some people have found better success with a rolling out method.

When you awaken in your sleep paralysis state, simply roll off the side of your bed. There is strong conditioning to avoid doing this because when you're awake, you've learned that falling off your bed usually results in pain, bumps, and bruises.

But rolling out of your body is done quickly, all at once, leaving your body wondering what the heck happened to you. You're sort of sneaking up on it and jumping out before it has a chance to keep you there.

When you roll out, your entire astral body is coming out at the same time, which helps you avoid that strong magnetic pull on your limbs. You're doing it all in one fell swoop.

However, rolling out of your body is not an easy method. It's effective for sure, but not easy. For one thing, when you roll out quickly, you may feel like you're falling. And that falling sensation is very primal, you'll instinctively jerk, which can cause you to snap back into your body.

But if you can get used to the sensation and actually like it, then rolling out is a great way to break free of the body quickly without having to coddle it and get its permission to let you out. I imagine it's how skydivers must feel after they've jumped out of airplanes many times. The falling sensation becomes a thrill instead of invoking panic.

If you achieve separation by rolling out of your body, you'll want to be careful not to continue your descent into your floor and then possibly the ground. It's disconcerting to project and find yourself immediately encased in tons of earth.

Once I got comfortable with astral projection, I would roll out of body and instantly take flight. If there was anything around me I didn't want to play with, then I would roll out, deliberately fly into the earth, and come up and out somewhere different. The entities didn't expect it, and it gave me the upper hand right away.

SINKING DOWN

Similar to rolling out, you can also try sinking down and exiting your body out the back, so to speak. So instead of stretching up and out, and instead of rolling quickly out and to the side, you're sinking down into your bed, through your floor, and then out.

The advantage of this technique is that it is a little easier to just let go and slip downward than it is to rise up. Same as if you were in a physical body, it's easier to let go and fall then it is to rise up or climb.

Another advantage is that it's easier to avoid the baddies when you slip out the back. Often they aren't expecting it and it takes them a while to recover and realize you're gone. By then you'll be far away and beyond their reach both "physically" and energetically.

One disadvantage is that you can accidentally sink to a lower vibration while in the process, so I only recommend the sinking technique if you've got a strong hold on your mind and your will is very strong. Also, you don't want to sink so low that you end up in the lower realms.

But if you can sink down and out, then take control, it's an effective way to slip out quickly and begin your travels.

TELEPORTING OUT

If you've tried stretching, rolling and sinking and just can't get free of your body without it snapping or pulling you back, then try teleporting out.

I discovered this technique accidentally. I had woken to sleep paralysis, got my buzzing and tingling going, had my dual vision, and was attempting to stretch up and out of my body, but it was hard, and I kept being pulled back. It suddenly occurred to me that if I was already in my astral vehicle, as evidenced by the separation sensations, then why did I have to obey the laws of physics and go from my body outward into the world? Why not just fold space and pop out in a new location?

So I gave it a try. I decided I wanted to be on the roof of my house, and willed myself there. When my astral vision caught up, I was floating above the roof of my house. It's instant freedom. You completely bypass the stretching and pulling and struggling and go right where you want to be.

Once I discovered I could do this, I did it a lot. Why go through the struggle when I could just pop out?

There are a few disadvantages to this method, however. First, when you teleport out, you need a very strong grasp on where you're going. You need to know it well so you can create a sort of anchor with it. If you decide to just teleport out of your body and let yourself land in a random location, you could arrive very disoriented and also land in a nest of things you don't want to play with.

I also found that I couldn't teleport too far away from my body. Maybe up to a block away from my house or starting location. I'm sure there are people out there who can teleport farther, but a block or so was my limit. I almost always just popped over to my roof because it was familiar to me and I could get to it easily.

Also, when you teleport out, you want to be sure that all of you is there when you arrive. Sometimes I ended up fragmented in some weird, twisted ways, and I'd have to go back to my body, gather myself up, and start again. My solution to that was to teleport to the same location, using it like a preset radio station. And I would wait a moment or two until all of me caught up. If I tried to teleport to other random locations, I'd have to pull myself together when I got there. It's like pieces of me stayed behind in my physical body and were stretching out to my current location. Not comfortable at all.

So this is again a case where you want to muster your will and intention and get all of you to your teleport location.

But the biggest advantage of this technique is that you don't struggle with the body. You pop out and you're free. The farther away you are from your physical body, the less gravitational pull you'll feel.

So if you're having trouble getting more than a limb or two out of your body, try teleporting out.

Getting Assistance

There is another way to achieve astral projection, and that's by allowing someone to help you out of your body. Once you've experienced astral projection, it's much easier to experience again. Just like when you were learning to swim, if someone held you up and prevented you from drowning while you got used to the water, it made it that much easier to learn, and you probably felt safer and more comfortable in the process. There are a couple ways to get assistance.

Spirit Guides. If you recall my first experience, I woke up in a state of sleep paralysis and then felt my soul being slowly pulled out of my body. It was frightening because I didn't know what was going on and I didn't know who the entities were that were assisting me. One even told me to breathe through my nose because it would be easier, and when I listened, I just got pulled out faster. I felt betrayed, so I struggled to get back into my body.

But what was actually happening was that I was receiving assistance from my own spirit guides in helping me astral project. If I had simply surrendered, I would have left my body, probably been fairly surprised, but not too upset, especially if they were able to reassure me that I was safe.

As the months passed, and I started to accept the fact that astral projection was finally upon me, after years of waiting for it to happen,

I started to trust my guides and my experiences, and let myself go. Once I did that, they were able to show me around the astral plane, help protect me, and help me reach new realms.

If you want your guides to help you, it's as simple as asking and allowing. Always put yourself in a nice high vibration before you speak to or communicate with your guides. Do this by meditating, doing some deep breathing, and imagining yourself walking up a long staircase in space that leads into a garden. Talk to your guides there.

If you can't visualize well, then meditate and simply talk to them in your mind. It can take some practice to make sure you're tuned in to your guides instead of your own imagination, but it's very possible. For articles and information on how to do this, visit my website, www.erinpavlina.com.

Even if you're not an expert at communicating with your guides, that's no problem. Simply tell them that you want assistance and that you're willing to allow it. They will hear you, and if they feel it's safe for you to project and that you're ready, they will likely assist you. Be ready. Prepare yourself. Do everything listed previously in this book to prepare yourself mentally, physically, and energetically. They can't throw you in the pool if you're not even standing near it. Meet them halfway by intending and preparing for the experience.

If you wake up in the sleep paralysis state, or if you're having difficulty getting out of your body, simply call out to your guides and ask them for assistance. Then prepare yourself for the experience, because it's likely going to be uncomfortable the first few times. Surrender to the experience, trust in your guides, and make sure you're not in a state of fear.

Friends. If your guides won't help you, perhaps your friends will. Someone who is astral projecting is capable of assisting someone else out of their body. Here's how that works.

When you are astral projecting, one of the things you will notice if you go visit other people, is that you'll often be able to see their astral bodies. It's like having X-ray vision and being able to see the peanut inside the shell. They're still inside their bodies, but you'll often see their astral bodies wiggling around in there. It's like they're lit up from the inside.

When I would project and fly down my hallway to see my parents, I often saw my mom's astral body staring back at me, even though her physical form was sound asleep on the bed. As I flew into the room, her astral body would watch me flying around. On some occasions, I would see her astral body a few inches outside of her body, but never fully out. I rarely saw my dad's astral body. It wasn't as active as my mom's.

Similarly, I could fly to a friend's house and see their astral body awake inside their physical ones. When I visited Jared and Ashley, I could see their astral bodies easily. They were bright and shiny lights sitting inside their bodies.

We discovered quite by accident that we could assist each other. I flew over to Ashley one night and simply reached my astral hand towards her head. As soon as I made contact, she would get some kind of energy burst, and pop out of her body. We were able to see each other, telepathically communicate with each other, and fly around together. It wasn't easy and it didn't always work. Sometimes I'd touch her, and she'd shrink back from the touch. It worked better if she was expecting me. And sometimes we'd start out together but drift apart, or one of us would slip into another plane and the other didn't follow.

One night I slept over Ashley's house, and we asked Sam to come visit us and take us out traveling with him, as he was way more accomplished at the time. I remember sometime in the early morning hours waking up and feeling his presence the way an intuitive person might sense a ghost. I said out loud, "Ashley, he's here!" and she responded in a sleepy voice, "Yeah, I know." I immediately settled onto my back and felt the tingling and high-pitched whine. I wasn't in sleep paralysis, so this was unusual. But Sam was reaching out to me and was able to activate my astral body so I could leave quickly and easily.

When I would try to coax other friends out of their bodies, I would simply hover nearby and telepathically project my thoughts at them. I would reassure them that they were safe, that I would protect them, and touch their energy with mine. Some friends and family made it out with me, and some didn't as they were too afraid.

This technique works much better when the person knows you're attempting it, and when the person you're assisting is practiced at initiating separation. So if you happen to have a close friend who is accomplished at astral travel, see if they can help pull you out of your body.

This does not work that well with strangers. If you don't recognize someone's energy, you may mistake it for a negative entity, especially if you're in a fear state. I've had numerous people ask me if they can pay me to come take them out of their bodies. It's not something I do unless I know the person very well. And even then, it's not as easy as it seems like it should be. There is a lot of resistance to overcome, same as if you're learning to project on your own.

But if you do have a close friend who is great at astral projection, ask them to try. Make sure you prepare yourself as best you can and make sure the conditions are as good as they can be.

DRUG-INDUCED ASTRAL PROJECTION

People often ask me if they can more easily achieve astral projection while under the influence of mind-altering drugs. I've received a lot of emails from people who had a "trip" that they felt was an out of body experience. I'm not a fan of using substances to create out of body experiences for several reasons.

First, depending on the substance you're using, what you believe is an astral experience may simply be a hallucination. How will you know if the experience you had was real or a figment of your hallucination? You won't know for sure. If you don't care about that and if you're comfortable just hallucinating, more power to you. But you'll never be sure if it was a real experience or just in your mind.

Second, if you do manage to achieve separation you're putting yourself at great risk. If you force an out of body experience, you may not be able to get back into your body too easily. And if you're surrounded by negative entities, you're going to want to get back in your body pronto. It's like walking outside to get some fresh air, getting swarmed by bees, and being unable to get back into your house because the door is closed.

Safe astral projection requires that you be in control of the duration of your experience. Don't allow yourself to be locked outside.

Third, many of these substances and drugs can have side effects that affect you physically. Is it worth damaging your body in order to have an out of body experience? True and natural astral projection won't eat away at your brain or body. It will energize and enhance you.

I've never done any drugs that would cause or create an out of body experience. For me the risk is too great. And after all the creatures I've sent packing, I can only imagine what they would do to me if I was thrown into jail with them and unable to end the experience when I wanted to. I shudder at the thought.

It's your choice, but I think if you practice and prepare yourself, you can achieve astral projection without drugs.

UNINTENTIONAL PROJECTIONS

Sometimes people unintentionally leave their bodies. Lucky, right? Not so. An unintentional projection is not what you're after because if you didn't initiate it, that means there's a problem. For something to knock your astral body out of your physical body, there had to be a glitch or a problem. Here are some examples.

While driving. Rare, but it happens. You can be in such a hypnotic state, super relaxed, and zoning out, maybe on a long drive, and pop. You're out of your body. Guess what? The car isn't going to drive itself. Without you being in your body, your physical body is going to go limp or collapse, which is not what you need while operating heavy machinery.

The way to avoid this is not to listen to any music that causes severe brain relaxation. Don't meditate while driving. And be sure you're not so tired that you can't drive consciously. If you do find yourself popping out of your body while driving, I suggest you pop yourself right back in!

During surgery or medical procedures. You may have heard about people under anesthesia reporting that they floated up out of their body while unconscious and could see and hear what their doctors were doing.

Sometimes when the body is in a twilight sleep or fully under, the astral body is unanchored and is free to roam. This can be bad news if you want to get back into your body. Usually people just hang out near their bodies and wait to go back in. Don't worry about this too much because there's no way to prevent it and you may not even remember if it happens.

During near-death experiences. You've probably also heard about near-death experiences, where the body is clinically dead and the person is moving on into the afterlife. In these cases, I believe the astral cord is still intact but wavering, as the connection prepares to sever forever. Or, the cord is severed but is somehow reconnected by beings on the other side who have decided it's not your time to die. I'm not really sure which, but this is an unintentional projection that often requires the assistance of other higher vibrational beings to get you back to your body.

While on drugs. Like I mentioned in the previous section, some drugs can pop you unintentionally out of your body. This puts you at great risk of being attacked by a negative entity. And sometimes you're not thinking clearly enough to use your will to fend them off or get back into your body. You're also more likely to wander, float away, or get pulled along by psychic wind, which we'll discuss later.

During accidents. Many years ago a friend told me that the day he got hit by a Mack truck, he popped out of his body instantly, and watched his body get thrown into the air and land many feet away. He was shocked to witness his own body being tossed about. A sudden impact can knock you out of your body, often for its own protection. Whether you get back in or not, depends on whether you live or not.

Randomly. I remember one time walking into my bedroom, early in the evening. I climbed into bed to watch TV and have a little snack. I felt a pop, and suddenly I was standing outside my body three feet away. I seriously thought I had died instantly somehow. I had no indicative sensations of astral projection. I had simply popped out. It was very unnerving. I looked around a bit, nothing was out of the ordinary, so I walked back to my body, lay down in it, and remerged with it. To this day I don't know what triggered that. If you find yourself out of your body randomly, I would get back in as soon as possible.

Part 4
Navigating the Astral Realms

CHAPTER 9
Traveling

You've made it out of your body. Congratulations! Now it's time to get moving. In the next three chapters you'll learn how to move your astral body, how to reach different planes of existence, and how to interact effectively with people and your environment once you are astral traveling. Your wild ride is about to begin!

Once you've successfully separated from your body, the first thing you'll want to do is start exploring and moving around. There is much you need to know about movement, so in this chapter I'm going to explain how to move through space, time, and objects. We'll also talk about how to control your speed, and some things that might knock you around a bit. Then we'll discuss how to quickly and safely return to your body.

METHODS OF MOVEMENT

There are several ways to move when you're astral. You can walk, fly, float, or teleport. You'll probably experience all four at some point, but eventually you'll pick the one you like the most and that's easiest for you. Let's discuss each method and how to master them all.

Walking. Walking is common because you're used to it. Some people step out of their bodies and simply walk around their house. When you walk, you move somewhat slowly, and you tend to follow the natural curvature of your space.

For example, if you get to some stairs, you're going to find yourself walking up or down the stairs like you would if you were corporeal. This is wholly unnecessary as you are actually on a plane that doesn't have stairs, but you see them, you're used to walking up or down them, so you force your astral body to mimic the movements as if you were physical.

If walking makes you comfortable, keep doing it, but eventually you'll probably want to go somewhere that you can't reach by walking. Imagine how long it would take you to walk to a friend's house three thousand miles away. Imagine how long it would take to climb a mountain step by step? Or harder yet, try walking to Mars.

So one disadvantage to walking is being limited by what you expect you can do physically. On the other hand, an advantage to walking is that it's easy and familiar, plus you can go slow and at your own pace, which allows you to explore in more depth and with more focus. But as a method of travel, it's definitely limited. If you're going to go far, you'll want to fly or teleport.

Floating. Once you've decided that walking is too limiting or too slow, you may decide you want to fly. So you get yourself into a horizontal position, and try to fly. But instead of flying, you find yourself floating, bobbing along through space like a two-day-old helium balloon.

It's extremely common to find yourself floating just a few inches or feet off the ground. Again, it's a perception. In your physical body, you don't fly or float, so it's sometimes hard to believe you can actually move without your feet touching the ground. Your own expectations or beliefs can create limitations that aren't really there.

Floating is an extremely slow method of movement. Probably the slowest. And it can cause great frustration because you want to move faster but can't seem to get going. But if you find yourself floating, unable to pick up speed, just enjoy the sensation and explore the area. In time, you'll get more confident about traveling out of your body, and you'll begin to pick up speed naturally. Floating will eventually lead to flying.

Flying. Most astral travelers eventually figure out how to fly, and this becomes the most common method of travel. When you can fly, it's much easier to soar into the sky and even into space. You can zoom quickly to locations halfway around the world. You can evade negative entities and leave them in your dust. You will have a sense of freedom and control the likes of which you have never experienced! In short, flying is awesome!

Tilt yourself into a horizontal position, put your arms out in front of you, and focus all your will and intent on your objective. You will begin to move in that direction. Your will and intent are critical. If you believe you are a bad-ass flying machine, you will be. If you're scared or tentative, you'll end up floating. Be confident, in control, and fierce. Pick a place you want to go and push your energy in that direction.

When I was first learning to fly, it helped if I took a few "running" steps first and launched myself into motion. It's a psychological trick, but it works. Another great way to learn to fly is to jump off your roof. You'll either fall really fast or learn to fly. It's exhilarating.

Once you're flying, you can fly high up in the sky, or stay low to the ground. When I was visiting friends, I often stayed low and flew near the ground so I could turn down the right streets. When I tried flying high up in the air and going to a friend's house, I had difficulty navigating and recognizing their rooftop from the crowd of rooftops I encountered.

But when I wanted to fly to far off locations, I went high up into the sky and zoomed around quickly, doing aerial feats along the way like somersaults and flips. It's addicting to be able to move your "body" in this way.

One disadvantage is that if you're flying too fast, you may miss some interesting details. But if your goal is to get somewhere quickly, flying is a fun and great way to go. Practice flying in your lucid dreams and you will be a pro when you go astral.

Teleporting. As I mentioned earlier, you can teleport out of your body, which also means that once you are astral, you can teleport to other locations around the globe. Just concentrate on where you want to be and pop yourself there.

Teleporting is mentally difficult. It's not something we're used to when corporeal, so your own mind may prevent you from achieving it. But if you practice, you can do it easily. Start by teleporting back and forth between two very familiar points, like your bedroom, and your street corner or roof.

When you teleport, sometimes it feels murky, and when you arrive at your destination, it can take a few moments to feel like you're all there. So if you're going to use teleportation as a method of travel, I recommend doing it one time per trip. Pick your spot, teleport there, then fly around and explore. If you teleport too much, you're going to become somewhat dissociated. If you find yourself in this situation, take a moment to collect yourself (literally), and then move again. If it's really bad, just snap back to your body and start again.

While teleporting is the fastest way to get to a new location, it's not the easiest method to master. Experiment with all the different travel methods until you find the one that works best for you and your needs.

Moving Through Time

Most people assume that when you astral project you'll fly around your area, your neighborhood, go see friends, check out Mars and maybe soar to the top of Mount Everest. And that's all well and good, and you'll have a great time doing it. But one of the more interesting things you can do while astral that you certainly can't do while corporeal, is time travel.

Imagine witnessing the creation of the universe. Imagine watching great historical moments with an unobstructed, unbiased viewpoint. What really happened behind closed doors during some of the most interesting political moments of our time?

Yes indeed, you can move yourself through time, not just space. Once you are astral, you are an energy being, completely unrestricted in terms of time and space. Time and space are for three-dimensional beings. You're now a four-dimensional being. Just as you can move through space, you can move through time.

And yes, that even means moving forward through time. But before you get too excited, let me explain the limitations, as there are a few.

First, if you thought moving through space was tough to get used to and master, you're going to have an even tougher time with time (excuse the pun). You're going to have to move in a way that is wholly foreign to you. You're going to need extreme focus and intent. And one thing you lose very quickly when you are astral, is extreme focus and intent.

When you go astral, you step back into your soul's energy. Your regular human problems and interests wane, and you become a point of consciousness moving around the cosmos. While your corporeal self may be very interested in how the dinosaurs really got wiped out, your astral soul consciousness may not care anymore. And if you don't have the will or the intent, you won't get where you want to go.

The best way around this is to concentrate really hard before you go astral and set the intention to visit a certain time, place or event in history. Then when you are astral, launch your "program" and teleport yourself to that time.

Moving through time is more difficult than moving through space. If you think it's disorienting to teleport your astral self from your bedroom to your roof, you're going to really be spinning when you try to teleport billions of years into the past. So don't be surprised if it doesn't work. Just keep trying.

The first time I discovered I could move through time, I was flying to Ashley's house. Along the way, I encountered a male spirit that wanted my attention. When he got close to me, he initiated something energetically and all of a sudden I found myself moving backward through time. It was flashing past me like a movie in rewind mode. He took me to a place roughly 30 years prior, and he showed me how he was in his house that caught fire and burned down, with him still in it. He showed me how he burned to death. I was watching as an observer. And he kept fast forwarding and rewinding the scene until I finally broke free of his hold and pulled myself back to the present. It wasn't the most pleasant experience, but I understood that he was confused and just wanted my help. I conveyed to him that he was dead and should move on, and then I left him because honestly I was a little afraid of him, but not the way I was afraid of negative entities from the lower planes.

After I realized I could witness past events, I started initiating them consciously. I would stand still, and send out my intention to the universe to be taken to various events. I didn't always succeed. Sometimes nothing would happen. Sometimes I'd start to experience that sensation of rewind, but stop or get stuck before getting to the right point. And sometimes I'd feel blocked from viewing something entirely. I could often hear an event but not see it. Very frustrating.

I came to understand that the more personal and psychological connection I had with an event, the more likely I was to be able to witness it. So I was taken back to my own past lives and witnessed many aspects of them. I found this to be awesome and interesting, so I'm grateful for the experiences.

I was also sometimes waylaid by spirits who wanted to show me their life or death. More about these experiences in Chapter 11.

Once I figured out I could go back in time, I tried to also go forward. I had some measure of success with this but was quite limited by my own expectations and blocks. Also, anytime I saw future events I understood intuitively that they were only *possible* events, and not set in stone.

I recall one instance in which I was taken to a time in the world when the entire planet was at peace and being ruled by a council of 13 people. I got an entire download of how the world was, and then like a flip book going backwards, I was shown how we got there as a planet. It was beautiful, but it moved so fast I couldn't consciously note exactly how it happened. By the time I was brought to the present, I knew only that it was possible and beautiful, but I couldn't consciously remember the steps we took to achieve it. Yeah, I was bummed. But I was also filled with incredible hope and the knowledge that there *is* a path to world peace and that it's possible. I hope if you practice time travel, you are successful at viewing everything you want to see.

When you want to get back to your body, sometimes it's easier to come back to the present and then step in. I found that to be the case for me. If I was in say 1969 and wanted to go back to my body, I would find myself in my bedroom but the 1969 version of it. Then I'd have to sort myself out from there. Very disorienting and confusing. You'll see what I mean when you're out there.

You may also want to know if you can affect past events. Not that I'm aware of. You are a witness only, an observer. Unless you were there corporeally, I don't believe you can affect past events. But sometimes being a witness is enough.

The other issue with time travel is that it's very hard to prove, unless you go back to a time and witness an event that you can then discuss with the people who were there, who can verify it for you.

Good luck in this endeavor. It's an interesting aspect of astral projection, and while it sounds powerful and awesome, I think you'll find when you get out there that what you think you'll be interested in viewing won't actually hold as much interest for you. But by all means, do what you will and explore away.

MOVING THROUGH OBJECTS

Once you're moving through space, you're going to run into some obstacles, or what appear to be obstacles. So let's discuss how to get through them and what it's going to feel like.

One of the first things I did when I went astral was attempt to fly outside my window and into the crisp, clear night. As I floated towards my window, I wondered how I was going to open it. I reached my hand out and was surprised to discover that my hand started to move through the window. It felt like I was pushing through some viscous liquid, but I got my hand through. Then I pulled my hand back. Same sensation. A thick liquid. I backed up a little and took a run at the window with more speed. I was able to fly through the window no problem, but as the window intersected with my astral body, it felt like I was moving through gel. There was resistance, but not much. Once I was outside, I felt whole again. Light. Airy. Intact.

I tried the same thing with my wall. Very thick. To me it felt like my energetic molecules were mixing with the atoms of the wall, and I had to keep pushing through quickly, or it felt like I might get stuck in the wall. It felt like my energy was merging with the wall's atomic make-up, and if I didn't keep moving through quickly, I might become part of the wall forever.

Here's what you need to know about moving through physical objects when you're astral. You can move through any object you see, but I don't recommend staying intersected with it for very long. It's an unusual sensation, not very comfortable, and just feels wrong. So when an object like a wall or window or tree is in your way, move through it quickly and keep on going.

I don't believe you could ever get truly stuck inside a physical object, but you are energy, the wall is energy, and if you stick around too long, you may find yourself experiencing what it's like to be wall atoms for a while. When you want to return to your body, coalesce your essence, and snap back into your body.

Once you become an expert at astral travel, you're going to realize the walls and other obstacles aren't really physical objects at all. They are just energetic representations of what is physically present on the three-dimensional plane. This is the reason that ghosts appear to walk through walls. It's because on that plane, the walls aren't even really there. You expect them to be, so you see them. In time, you'll zip through walls and windows like they were air.

Some people get hung up on trying to get through an object because their mind is telling them it's impossible to move through something solid. If you find it difficult to get through the wall or window easily and quickly, it helps to focus on what's beyond the object and move towards that. Then the wall or window don't even come into play.

SPEEDING UP

One of the most common questions I'm asked about motion is how to speed up. It's not much fun to float and bobble along at a snail's pace when you're trying to reach something wonderful before you're snapped back, or when you're trying to escape something that's faster than you. Imagine being a balloon trying to swim away from an attacking shark! Speed is important to master when you're astral.

The trick with speed is time, practice, patience, and will. First, you will absolutely get faster over time. The more you project and the more experience you have with flight and movement, the faster you will become naturally. So worst case scenario, you will eventually speed up the more times you travel.

Practice makes perfect. If you don't practice your flying, you'll move slowly for a long time. If you're working on or mastering lucid dreaming, practice flying in your dreams. You're going to use the same motions during astral travel. If you have the reference experience of knowing what it feels like to fly during dreams, you'll be much faster at speeding up once you're astral traveling.

Patience is key, as well. Don't give up in frustration. Flying quickly will happen at some point. It might come when you're very scared and absolutely *need* to get away from something. It might happen when your desire to get something awesome overcomes your fear, conditioning, or reluctance to travel, but if you keep projecting and you keep trying, you'll get it.

And lastly, your will is very important. When you're on the astral plane, what you resonate with is what you'll experience. If you believe you can fly fast, you will fly fast. If you take limited thinking with you to the astral plane, you'll continue to bob along a few feet off the ground, even with time, practice, and patience. Your belief will create the reality.

When I was first learning to project, I was already very accomplished at lucid dreaming, and flying was second nature to me. It didn't take me very long on the astral plane to discover that I could fly like Superman. In fact, there came a point when I wanted to see just how fast I could fly, and I'm pretty sure you'd have clocked me at several hundred miles per hour. You can probably warp yourself to light speed and beyond, as well. I never found that necessary, but I'm sure it's possible.

Speed flying is an awesome sensation. I highly recommend it. And there are no police officers around to ticket you for speeding. Bonus!

Astral Wind

I discovered astral wind quite by accident. I'd left my body, flew out of my bedroom window, and started flying to Ashley's house. I was tooling along at a nice clip when all of a sudden I felt a wind come up and blow at me. I found myself tumbling uncontrollably down a street. I felt like an astral tumbleweed. It took me more minutes than I'd like to confess to right myself, get in control of my movement, and get back on my trajectory.

The next day I talked to Sam about it (Oh how I wish Google or the Internet had existed back then!) and we went to the library to see if we could find any reference to this experience in any books. Remember, the number of books even mentioning astral projection was so limited, but eventually we found something that referred to psychic wind. And sure enough, it was described as the sensation of being blown around the astral plane like you were a leaf on a windy day.

We further read that it was not an attack. Even though it sort of felt like something was shoving me around, it's not a conscious entity trying to knock you down or get control of you, any more than wind is trying to kill you.

In fact, the psychic wind seemed as relatively harmless as a light breeze on a summer day. But what if the wind turned into hurricane force gales? If you ever find yourself completely out of control and unable to direct your course, you can always snap back to your body. Then you can stop for the night or try moving out again.

I don't think you're going to encounter the astral wind very often, if ever. I only encountered it two or three times out of a thousand flights, so it's really not a big concern, but I wanted to mention it in case you do experience it, so you're not overly troubled by it.

RETURNING TO YOUR BODY

Another big question people ask me is, "How do I get back into my body when I want to? Is there a chance I won't be able to get back in?"

Let me reassure you about this. When you astral travel, you are still very much alive, you're merely taking a temporary journey outside of your body. Just like in physical reality, when you take a trip, you come home and your house is still there, and it's still yours, and you can still get in, that's how it is with astral travel. Your astral cord acts as a placeholder or bookmark, holding your spot for when you're ready to return.

There are only two reasons you wouldn't be able to get back into your body. The first is if something severs your astral cord. In our physical reality trip analogy, that would be like losing your key. Your house is still there, but you no longer have access to it. What can sever your cord? Only something ridiculously powerful that desires to end your life that can also get past your guides, angels, and the Source.

The second reason you may not get back is if something kills your physical body, which will snap your cord by default. That's like coming home from Aruba and finding your house got bulldozed to make way for a hyperspace bypass. You've still got the key, but there's no lock because there's no more house. What can kill your physical body while you're astral? Anything really. Earthquake knocks tons of rubble onto your bed. You're dead. Someone walks in your room and shoots you in the head. You're dead. But it's not any more likely to happen while you're astral than when you're not.

No being can step into your body while you are projecting and take it from you, leaving you floating along behind it, knocking on your skull to get back in. Nothing.

Now let's talk about how to return to your body. For the most part, all you have to do is think about being back in your body and you'll get there. You'll snap right back. Your body is happy to recall you back to base any time you're willing to come back.

But sometimes an entity may try to mess with your mind. I recall a lovely incident when I was roaming astrally and a pretty bad-ass vampire-looking thing was standing between me and my body when I got back to it. It hissed at me, "Are you sure you want to go back to your body?" I replied, "Yes, God damn you!" It recoiled like I hit it with holy water and dissipated. I then got back into my body. Was I scared? Uh, yeah, a little bit, but I also recognized that it could not prevent me if I really wanted to go back. If necessary, I could have gotten back into my body without lashing out at him first.

Another easy way of getting back into your body is to fall. The sensation of falling creates a primal instinct in your body that will snap you back really fast. Simply fly to a tall place high in the sky or on top of a mountain and throw yourself off. It's even more effective if you fall backwards. Snap! You'll be back in your body before you can count to one. This doesn't work too well if you enjoy the sensation of falling or you get too used to it, which is what happened to me over time. I would simply fall, "hit" the earth and keep falling into the core.

You can also simply fly back to your body and step in. You'll see your body lying on your bed or couch, looking all peaceful and content. Just lie down right on top of it and feel yourself merge back into place. In a few moments, you'll be reconnected, and you'll open your physical eyes and be back. It's very gentle, and a preferred method for those who hate the sensation of snapping back to their bodies. Experiment to find what works best for you. In Chapter 13 we'll talk more about what to do when a negative entity tries to prevent you from returning, but for now just know that nothing can stand in the way of you moving back into your body.

CHAPTER 10

The Planes

A lot of people assume that when you astral project you just fly around your house, visit friends, and go spy on celebrities. There's a lot more to it than that. You become an energy being, and physical limitations are a thing of the past. There are many planes you can explore. Let's talk options!

PRIME MATERIAL PLANE

The first plane is referred to as the prime material plane. I don't know if that's what scientists call it, but that's what it's called in my astral social circles. The prime material plane is simply the three-dimensional plane you live in. It's the plane you're on right now. It's generally viewed as quite physical, full of matter and solid objects. In reality we know that solid objects are made up of energy and space, but let's set that aside for now and just refer to this plane we're living on as the prime material plane.

When you first project, you're generally going to find yourself as an astral being on the prime material plane. In other words, when you step out of your body you'll still be in your bedroom or house. You can fly down your hallway. You can tear off down the street and go explore the world. All the physical things you're familiar with and expect to see, you will see. You are an energetic being intersecting with the prime material plane.

Some people never go beyond this plane and that's fine. There is a lot to explore. You will visit obvious places like your house, your family and friends, and your neighborhood. But you can also go where you've never physically gone before. You can fly to the top of a tall mountain, swim into the depths of the ocean, explore caves, the pyramids, look for Atlantis. You can soar into the sky. You can time travel through the prime material plane. It's rich with interest.

When you're ready, though, pack your astral bags, because there are other planes to explore!

THE LOWER PLANES

I'm no physicist, so my explanation of planes is coming from a place of subjective experience only. What I refer to as the lower planes are simply the planes where lower vibrational beings reside. Think of the planes as frequencies on a radio. The lower planes are simply a band of frequencies on the lower end of the scale.

You can visit the lower planes if you want to, but I don't really recommend it. The lower planes are where you're going to find lower vibrational beings. I don't know what they call themselves, but around here we refer to them as energy vampires, demons, ookie spookies, negative entities, and lower vibrational beings. But hey, everyone needs someplace to live, right?

If you slip into the lower planes, you're going to almost assuredly be attacked or swarmed by these beings. They're going to see you as a tasty snack and feed on your light. This will result in you going back to your body with a feeling of malaise and low energy. Imagine how you'd feel if someone drained half the blood out of your body. That's what it will feel like when these guys are done with you.

So how do you get to the lower planes? If your vibration is negative or fearful, you could slip down there. This means you're emanating fear, anger, anxiety, sadness, grief, shame, or guilt. You shouldn't be projecting at all if this is your dominant energy.

Another way to get to a lower plane is to be dragged there. We'll talk more in Chapter 13 about what happens when you are wrongfully and willfully attacked by one of these fellows and how to escape them, but for now it's important to know that if you're not careful and you're not totally in control, you could be dragged against your will to the hellish planes.

Another method to visit the lower planes is to go there on purpose. I used to go there a lot. Not because I was in a low vibration, but because I was sick and tired of the ookie spookies trying to attack me and feed off my energy, so sometimes I'd go hunting there on purpose, and I'd stab lower vibrational entities with my light sword. You'll learn about that soon. Sometimes I would follow a nasty back to its proverbial lair, and send it so much love energy that it would scurry away like a cockroach in the light. That was fun for me, and how I got my kicks on the astral plane when I was a teenager.

So you can consciously or unconsciously go to the lower planes. I'm here to tell you, though, that you can astral project thousands of times and never go to the lower planes. It's simply unnecessary and not recommended. If you're afraid to project because you're afraid you'll end up there, don't be afraid. By the time you finish this book, you'll have the tools and knowledge necessary to avoid the lower planes altogether, and you'll know how to get out of them if you end up there against your will.

You also need to know that nothing can keep you in the lower planes against your will. You can always snap back to your body. And assistance is always close by. More on that soon.

Keeping your vibration high will keep you from slipping into the lower planes, and will prevent negative energies from kidnapping and dragging you there. High vibration energies are love, compassion, gratitude, and joy. If you're projecting in that state, you'll never see the lower planes.

Reaching the Higher Planes

The antithesis to the lower planes is what I call the higher planes or the higher realms. It is here that you will encounter other four-dimensional beings including spirit guides, angels, deceased loved ones, ascended masters, and even God or Source itself. That's right, the party is in the heavens and the upper planes! How do you get your ticket to ride? Your vibration is your pass. That, and your intention and desires.

When I first began projecting, I was in a state of fear most of the time. This was partly because my first projection was forced, and then Jared told me the entities were trying to possess me. You'd be scared too! So in the beginning, when I stepped out of my body onto the prime material plane, I'd encounter or be attacked by the lower vibrational entities. They'd drag me around, feed on me, scare the crap out of me, and I'd end up back in my body tired, scared, and flipped out of my mind.

It wasn't until I started talking with Sam and learned about the different planes and the different opportunities that awaited me that I started having positive experiences. One of these experiences was reaching the higher planes. Here's what happened.

Sam had told me the next time I found myself in sleep paralysis and beginning to tingle, to call out to my spirit guides and ask them to guide and assist me on my astral journeys. I'm not sure at the time I was super clear on what a spirit guide was, but I knew they were assigned to us at birth and were there to guide us and help us navigate the maze of our lives.

So there I was, tingling, dual vision, hearing the high-pitched whine, and beginning to feel and hear the usual suspects crowding around my body just waiting for me to leave so they could eat me, and instead of stepping out of my body, I silently and telepathically called out, "Guides? Come help me." I felt a whoosh of air around me. It was like the hand of some mighty being swished away all the bugs. I could sense the area was clear. Then I felt a hand grab onto me and pull me out of my body. I saw a being of light next to me, radiating strength, power, and positive energy. Its masculine energy said, "Where would you like to go?" I replied, "Just show me around and let me see what you think I should see."

Thus began one of the most wonderful and positive astral experiences I've ever had. I was taken to the higher realms. I interacted with deceased people. I connected with angels, ascended masters. I saw beauty that went so far beyond the physical that it would have brought tears to my eyes if I had them with me. I was in a state of communion with Source. I was introduced to celestial beings that weren't even human. It filled me with such positive energy that when my guide dropped me back into my body, I came back to the physical with more energy than I'd started. Yes! Now this is what I wanted! More, more, more!

Once I learned the frequency of the higher realms, I visited them often. I explored small areas in great detail. Sometimes I was denied entry to certain places. A friendly cuff on the astral ear would send me scurrying. Sometimes I encountered pockets of beings interacting with each other, and sometimes they'd let me into their "conversations." At times I felt like I was eavesdropping on creation, but I was mesmerized by the workings and energetic interplay of these beings. As long as I kept my vibration high, I could reach them. This became easier to do over time.

If you want to experience these realms, you can. You are allowed. But you must keep your vibration high, or you will be unable to connect with them. You can ask your guides, higher self, and angels for assistance. Avail yourself of your helpers and your posse on the other side.

Some people ask me how you know if these "guides" are positive energy beings or just negative entities masquerading as guides. You will feel it. When you are astral, you can see energy and gauge it clearly. Your gut instincts will tell you whether something is truly good or not.

THE ASTRAL HIGHWAY

What connects all the different planes together? It's generally referred to as the astral highway. It's the place of energetic intersections with astral roads that can take you from one end of the spectrum to the other.

Think of it like a freeway system, with on-ramps, exits, and miles of roads in between. Travelers use it to go from one plane to another. It's a very busy place in some areas, and other areas are not well traveled.

You don't need to worry about the astral highway very much. You're either going to be passing through it, largely unaware of it as you zip off to your next destination, or you may decide to stop and interact with other travelers on the highway.

It's not more safe or dangerous than a real highway. You'll want to use your intuition to determine if any beings you might be interacting with are of a high vibration or a low vibration. But it's a great place to interact with other beings.

In my travels, when I bothered to just stop and see what's around me, I met a vast array of beings, many of them non-human, who reside on one plane or another and are moving around out there. I couldn't always communicate with them, but I was aware of their presence and received some information about who they were and what they were about. Think of it like going to an astral bar and meeting new people.

If you want to go there, my advice is to simply intend to go there. Like I said, you're using the connectors anyway, usually without realizing it. So it's really a matter of just stopping and staying still so you can perceive what else is around you. I highly recommend you only do this when you're in a high vibration. If you need or want assistance, ask your guides to take you there and babysit you, so you don't make a social faux passé and get metaphorically slapped in the face.

EXPLORING THE GALAXY

When I first started projecting regularly, I got pretty comfortable with my routine. Leave the house, visit friends, try to pull them out of their bodies, and play around the neighborhood. Then I got interested in seeing how far I could go, so I started traveling the planet. I even went overseas. I thought I was a total bad ass world traveler. Then one day I got an offer.

I was getting ready to project and noticed there were two beings in my room with me. Both felt masculine. One of them projected into my mind, "Would you like to go visit the moon?"

The moon? Really? That's possible? I replied tentatively, "Uh yeah, sure, that sounds like fun."

He replied, "Okay, but we'll have to get past the guard dogs first."

I immediately got the prickle up my spine that told me these dudes were up to no good. I knew if I took their "hands" they would snatch me away someplace not at all good. Always trust your intuition when you're astral.

I pulled away from these guys and called upon my guides to help me. I heard the beings cackling as they left. Not cool. I was young and inexperienced at that point and quite gullible. But it got me thinking. Could I go to the real moon? Could I even visit other planets? Could I explore the universe?

I talked about it with Sam, and he agreed it must be possible since planets and stars were part of the prime material plane. I decided to give it a shot. I wondered if my astral cord would stretch that far and was a little nervous about being so stretched and far from my body. I felt vulnerable to attack. This of course put me in a low vibration, and I didn't get very far before having to defend myself from the ookie spookies.

The next time I wanted to try it, I asked my guides to take me on a journey through the cosmos. And journey we did. They whisked me to other planets, some in our solar system and some obviously outside of it. I don't think there's any way I could have gotten myself to these places on my own, so I highly recommend that if you want to try this that you book travel with your spirit guides. I felt safe the entire time, which left me free to just enjoy the journey.

I ended up at the moon many times, and my fascination with Mars put me in proximity to it, as well. There wasn't a whole lot to do or see though and I didn't spend a lot of time exploring the galaxy, but if that's something you desire to do, you can definitely do it when you're astral. The farther away you move from your body, however, the more vulnerable you may feel. Godspeed to you though!

You don't need to worry about whether your astral cord can sever while you're out so far. It's a tough little bugger and it can stretch farther than you can imagine.

CHAPTER 11

Interacting with People and the Environment

Now that you're moving around in time and space, soaring to new heights, and visiting all the planes and realms you can find, it's time to learn how to interact capably and effectively with the beings you meet and the environments you land in.

HOW THINGS LOOK AND SOUND

One of the first things you're going to notice when you step out of your body is that you can still see and hear, even though your eyes, ears, and brain are back in your body. You are just pure consciousness, tethered energetically to your body and your identity. I heard recently that people who are born blind are able to see during near death experiences. That doesn't surprise me because when we slough off this mortal coil we are whole and complete, and we can hear and see even without a body.

When you first step out of your body and are standing on the prime material plane you're going to look around the room and, generally, it will look like it normally does. You'll see your bed, your door, your closet, your lamp or clock, etc. But don't be surprised if there are some things missing. I'm not sure why this happens, but sometimes when I'd go astral, some of the items in my room disappeared visually. I suspect this is because matter is energy vibrating at a certain frequency or speed, and when we are on a different plane, not everything is perceptible.

I also think our expectations can manifest what we want to see or expect to see, which may account for me seeing a few extra things on the astral plane that are not perceptible to me when I am in my physical body. Experiment with your reality and see what you see.

Your hearing on the astral plane is usually much sharper than when you are physical. You will hear noises and sounds that are unusual, and even seem to be coming from a different plane altogether. Hearing feels very non-linear on the astral plane. It's like being able to hear many radio stations at the same time. You have to learn to sort through them, focus on what you want to hear, and stay tuned in to that frequency. This will get easier with practice.

Don't be surprised if you hear sounds that are loud and sharp, or even sounds that are static. It will sort itself out as you get going and as you get used to being in the astral state.

One phenomenon that happens often is having cloudy vision. You go astral, expecting to be able to see just fine, but it's like looking through layers of cloth. Your vision is obscured, like trying to look through opaque stained-glass. Nothing is sharp. It's very frustrating.

Sometimes the vision clears up, and sometimes it doesn't, and your entire trip is visually impaired. I found the best way to clear my vision was to merge back in with my body and step out again. Some people experience visual cloudiness when they teleport out of their bodies. I hope one day science can give a good explanation for why this happens, but at this point, it's something to be aware of and to accept. But don't let it alarm you if you go astral and can't see very well.

Affecting the Environment

Can you affect your physical environment when you are astral projecting? I get this question frequently. Yes, you can alter the physical environment, but it is ridiculously difficult to do, especially in the beginning.

You are like a ghost, traveling through your home, moving through walls and solid objects. How will you get a hold of one of those objects and move it? With what hands will you grasp it? With no physical body, you can't just grab something and move it around.

Instead, you're going to have to interact with its energy. And then you're going to have to convince it to move. And because it's not a sentient, conscious being, that's going to be tough.

I only managed to affect my physical environment twice that I can recall. In one instance I remember being very cold in the middle of the night. I left my body, flew downstairs, hovered in front of the thermostat dial and willed it to move. I remember watching the dial spin all the way counter-clockwise. Then I flew back to my body and got back inside. In the morning my father said at breakfast, "Who turned the thermostat all the way to the 90s? It sure got hot last night!" Realizing that it must have been me, I began to experiment with affecting the physical environment, imagining all kinds of useful and fun things to play with.

I tried using my will on an object, "Move, damnit, move!" No movement. I tried reaching my ghostly hand into an object, but all that did was merge my energy with the object and feel weird. I tried pushing it with my mind. Nothing. It seemed as if trying to use physical methods of motion while in an energetic state was not conducive to success.

Next I tried changing my reality. I put a necklace on my nightstand, and when I went astral I looked very carefully at the necklace, trying to wrap my mind around its energy and existence. Then I imagined it being on the floor. I expected it to be on the floor. I knew it was on the floor, and when I looked again, hey, it was on the floor! When I got back to my body and got out of bed, the necklace was on the floor. I felt like I had reprogrammed its location in the matrix.

I never spent much time working on this because it took a ton of time and energy and didn't gain me much. Frankly, it wasn't that interesting. But try it for yourself and see what you can move or reprogram. I'd love to hear about your experiences with this. If ghosts can learn to move photographs, and if poltergeists can toss furniture across the room, there's got to be a way for astral travelers to do it too.

VISITING SPECIFIC PEOPLE

One of the most enjoyable activities to engage in when you're astral projecting is visiting people you know. There's a natural inclination to want to stand in front of someone while you're astral and jump up and down, waving your arms, to see if they can see you and hear you.

Also, it's really fascinating to see the energies in physical people while you're astral. I mentioned earlier that sometimes I'd see my mom's astral body awake inside her physical one, staring at me, sometimes in surprise, sometimes in delight. So what is the best way to visit people, and what can do you when you get there?

Pick a friend, any friend. The first thing to do, in advance if possible, is decide whom you're going to visit. Deciding in advance is important because once you're astral you can sometimes be distracted by other things going on around you and forget what you wanted to do. If you know in advance what you want to do and whom you want to visit, you'll be more likely to remember it when you're astral.

If you live with other people, it's going to be pretty easy to move to their bedroom to see them, so in the beginning you might want to pick someone in the same house as you. If you live alone, pick a specific person you'd like to visit. I highly recommend you pick someone in close proximity to your starting location because you can easily get distracted or blown off course as you travel to them.

Go to them. Once you are astral, use your preferred method of travel to get to your friend's physical location, whether that is just down the hallway, or down a few blocks. If you have to go to another city, I recommend teleportation if you're familiar enough with their room to be able to pinpoint it. Otherwise, flying is fast and keeps you on track visually. But the farther you have to go, the more chance you will get distracted, attacked, blown around by psychic wind, or simply lose your way. When was the last time you accurately flew three hundred miles without a compass or an airplane?

Concentrate on their energy. What if your friend isn't home? What if they aren't even in their bedroom? If you project during the day, or if there is a significant time difference between you and your intended, you may not find them in their bedroom sleeping peacefully. In that case, you must seek them out energetically.

I had to do this many times with my friends because I often projected during a midday snooze. Once you're out of your body, simply concentrate on their energy. Will yourself to go to them. You may feel yourself pulled along by some invisible tether, or you may find yourself teleporting to their current location. All it takes is thought. Think about your friend, and you will get there.

Watch out for shields and guardians. If your friends are accomplished at astral projection, chances are they have set up shields or guardians around their bodies. Guess what happens when you try to visit someone with a shield or guardian. Sometimes you get repelled or snapped back to your body.

The first time I discovered this was even possible was one night when I got out of my body and decided to visit Sam. I was elated that I remembered my goal, and I was even more pleased that I made it to his house, but I wasn't prepared for what greeted me.

I got to his room and it was dark. I approached his bed so I could touch him astrally, wake him up, and see if he wanted to travel with me, but I was met by two red eyes and a growl. *Holy hell hound, Batman! What the heck is that?* A creature that looked marginally like a bulldog came at me. I backed up immediately. I remember trying to reason with the animal, to reassure it that I was a friend of Sam's, but it just kept growling at me. Eventually, it latched on to my astral arm and pulled me away from Sam. I left, deflated and dejected to be so close to my goal and run into this astral mutt.

In the morning I told Sam that I tried to visit him but ran into this creature. Sam chuckled and said, "Ah, you met my guard dog." In the next chapter, I'll explain how to set up guardians and shields. For now, you need to make sure that whoever you're visiting wants to be visited, and you need to remember that if you can guard your body while you're gone, so can other people.

Make advance arrangements. The best way I found for connecting with friends was simply to tell them I was coming and to expect me. This worked even better once I had mastered astral travel and was able to leave at will. In the beginning, you may not have enough control over your projections to reliably make it to a friend's house on the night you say you're going to. Just let them know you might be coming for a visit and that you mean them no harm. If they have shields or guardians they'll be able to call off the guardians or lower the shield when your energy comes knocking.

Be respectful. I hope it goes without saying, but be respectful of others. When you go visit your friends, don't spy on them in the shower or while they are undressing. This goes for visiting strangers as well. Character is how you behave when no one else is watching. Treat others as you would want to be treated. Sometimes people who are awake can feel someone else in the room with them if they are intuitive or sensitive. You're going to seriously creep them out if you're standing next to them. Now if you have permission, go for it. It will be fun to see if they notice you when you are actually there.

People ask me whether you can use astral projection to spy. Yeah, technically you can. When you're astral you have the opportunity to go anywhere on this planet. You could go see what the president of the United States is doing. If you got good enough at astral projection, you could conceivably sell your spy services to the government. But you're more likely to find you don't have a real interest in that kind of work and can't do it reliably enough to be useful.

You could go visit a celebrity. I once found myself floating around a birthday party on a Saturday afternoon that a famous celebrity couple was throwing for their son. I remember wanting to see what their house was like so I flew in and wandered around the rooms. That's when I saw the male partner canoodling with a woman who was not his spouse! I was so shocked. I just stood there for a moment, then I pulled myself away. I remember thinking, "Wow, this couple is viewed as extremely close and faithful to each other, one of the few Hollywood couples who are making it work." It bugged me for years, and then I found out recently that the couple has a "don't ask, don't tell" policy when it comes to extramarital affairs. Maybe that's how they're making it work in Hollywood.

When I was a teenager and projecting frequently, I did visit as many of my celebrity crushes as I could. I'm not overly proud of this, but I did it. But you know what? It's not terribly interesting watching them sleep, or walking around unable to make them aware of your presence. I soon got tired of that.

Set up experiments. Here's something you can try. Ask a friend to take a card out of a deck and lay it face up on a table. Then astral project to their house and look at it. In the morning, tell them what card you saw. There should be a fair degree of accuracy in this, but sometimes you can be obfuscated. Here's what can knock you off course…

First, remember that when you're astral, you lose a lot of interest in things that your corporeal self might be interested in. So you may not care to go look at the card.

Second, you may get to their room, but have cloudy vision and be unable to see it clearly. If the room is too dark, you may also not be able to make out which card it is. See if they can set up a nightlight with low wattage near the card.

Third, the card may morph, which is something I've seen physical objects do, especially when you're trying to view them closely.

There are other games you can play that are often easier though. A playing card is small. Instead, have your friend put a large piece of paper on their wall with a number on it or a drawing of an object. The bigger the better. Keep it simple. You can also ask them to put a larger object in a special pre-arranged location and tell them what object you saw when you arrive.

Do this enough and you'll probably convince people that astral projection is real, and maybe they'll even want to learn it themselves. Do it for science, do it for the fun! Think of other games to play and enjoy yourself!

TRAVELING WITH OTHERS

Visiting friends is fun, but traveling with friends is even more interesting. Sam came and pulled me out of my body in the beginning. He taught me a little about how to do it and maintain the connection. Then I started arranging to travel with Jared and Ashley.

I never pulled someone out of their body against their will. You will scare the bejesus out of them. Just like my first experience when my guides were pulling me out of my body, it nearly scarred me for life. Be respectful!

Sometimes, in my travels I would see people partly out of their bodies, or hovering inside their bodies, and I knew I could go over and gently guide them out. But I still never did it. It didn't feel right to me. As I would approach them, they would emanate a fear vibe like an animal backed into a corner, and I would back off until they calmed down again, and then go on my merry way.

When you decide you want to travel with someone, try to select someone who is already accomplished at astral projection or wants to learn it and is willing to give you permission to pull them out. I can't stress this enough. Be gentle. This is a soul you're playing with.

Assuming you've found a willing travel partner, here's what you need to know to travel together safely.

It's difficult. Meeting up on the astral plane is not easy. There are a lot of pieces to get right in order for this to work. You have to astral project at the same time, on the same plane, and at the same frequency. There are a lot of factors that are in your control and a few that are not, so you want to maximize your chance of success.

Arrange a time. Discuss with your intended partner what day you will attempt it. Then make sure you know what time of the day to project. If you're in the same time zone and you both prefer projecting at sunrise, you've got it made. But if your partner is half a world away, one of you will be projecting during the day and one of you at night, so make sure you've got your time zones worked out and that you know when the attempt will be made.

Jared, Ashley, and I all lived within a few miles of each other, so that was easy to arrange. But sometimes one of us would project at 12:45 a.m. and the other wasn't able to initiate separation until 4 a.m., and we'd miss our rendezvous. This is why being an advanced student will help you because you'll be able to initiate your separation when you want to. Still, if you go to sleep first, you may completely sleep through the appointed time. It was often hit and miss with me and my friends, but you try enough times, and you'll eventually succeed.

Pick a location with a strong anchor. When we first attempted to meet up on the astral plane, we'd pick a location like the lamppost on the corner to meet up. It was easy for me to get to because it was right outside my house, but Ashley or Jared had to fly miles to get there and would often get distracted or run out of time before they got there.

Then we decided we'd meet up at our high school parking lot because it was a location with a strong energetic connection. That worked fairly well. We were all familiar with the energy because it's where we spent most of our days. But still some nights we'd become distracted and couldn't meet up.

What we found worked best was for one person to project and then go pick up the others from their bodies directly. That took care of the time and location problem in one fell swoop. So we knew what night we were planning to do it, and whoever got out of their body first would simply go to the others' bedroom and initiate a wake-up.

This won't work well if you have never been to your partner's physical location. I'm not saying it can't work, just that it's going to be more difficult if you don't have a strong energetic connection to that location. You'll instead focus on the person's energy and use your love and care for them as your energetic anchor. Think of them, and go to them.

Sleep in the same room. If possible, be in the same room with your travel partner ahead of time. Then the distance between you is gone. Slip out of your body and you're right there beside them already. There's much less time for you to become distracted or knocked off course. Sometimes if I was spending the night at Ashley's house we would meditate before bed, which helped sync our energies, and raise our vibrations. That seemed to increase our success on nights we did that.

Knock, knock. So you've picked a time, date, and location, and you're ready to rock and roll. Exit your body and fly, teleport, or walk to your partner's body. Their astral body may be looking at you when you arrive. You'll see it as an ethereal, energetic version of them that is not remotely asleep or unconscious. It will look alert and possibly frightened.

With Ashley and Jared, seeing my astral form by their bed was often enough to trigger them to project. But if you're working with someone who is new to this, gently reach your astral hand out to them and touch them lightly. Sometimes touching the head triggers a connection and sometimes you just need to touch their hand or arm. Send out reassuring thoughts of love and care. "It's me, I'm here, you're safe. Come on out."

If the person is scared, they likely won't come out. But if you've discussed travel ahead of time, and if they remember they agreed to do this, you'll probably be able to coax them out. Remember that the sensations they are feeling might scare them. They're going to have sleep paralysis, dual vision, tingling, and buzzing. Continue to gently reassure and coax until they release from their body. Obviously trust is important here.

Once they are out, you should be able to see each other. If not, you'll feel their presence around you. The first challenge is accomplished, getting out of the body at the same time and in the same place. Now the next challenge comes into play.

Staying together. Remember all those different planes? Which one will you travel on? How will you convey that to your partner? What if you lose each other? How will you get back together?

Jared, Ashley, and I quickly found that going astral at the same time and place was the easy part. Staying together was harder. As we'd begin flying off together, sometimes one of us would slip off the prime material plane and onto a higher or lower plane. We couldn't always find each other when that happened.

We learned that we had to sync our frequencies. It's like creating a preset station on a radio. We'd tune in to each other's energy before flying off together. Or we'd create an energetic tether between us. It also helped if we designated one person as the leader and the others are followers. Then we allowed ourselves to be pulled or dragged along with our leader. It helped us stay together.

It seemed to work best if we stayed on the prime material plane, which is the plane that was most familiar to us. You can communicate telepathically with your partner(s). It just takes some practice.

Reconnecting. If you do lose each other, you can reconnect. Again it's all about will and intention. The better you know your partner, the more easily you'll recognize their energy signature and frequency. Practice stopping, tuning in, and pulling them back to your location, or finding and going to them directly. It's very easy to lose track of each other on the astral plane, so this will take time, practice, and patience. Keep at it.

Sometimes if I lost Jared or Ashley, we would just agree to meet back in one of our bedrooms and start again. Most of our journeys lasted just a few minutes, but there were some that lasted much longer. We also managed to attract the attention of something very mean and nasty which had to be dealt with. More on that in Chapter 13. Let's just say for now that we were a big cluster of bright shiny lights emanating a lot of power, and a lot of things wanted to take a bite out of us.

Coming back. When you're done traveling, you can just disengage from each other and allow yourself to snap back to your body, or you can continue traveling on your own. Totally up to you. It's best to disconnect consciously though, otherwise your energy can get tangled up, and you'll probably end up with a headache or a sore body as you move throughout your day.

What do you even do out there? Once we got together, maintaining the connection was pretty tough, so usually we would fly around a bit and go home. As time went on, we started to be able to visit other planes while we were still together. If we lost each other, we'd just wait for the other person to catch up.

In time, we would encounter other beings or other groups. Some were nice, and some would attack us. We learned how to fight together, and we learned how to commune with higher vibrational beings together. You and your travel partner will find your way. Experiment. A lot.

The day after a mutually shared projection experience we would discuss what happened. Since we all remembered the same details, we knew it was real and that it really happened.

ASTRAL SEX

There are other connections you can make during astral travel, and I would be remiss if I didn't mention it and make you aware of the joys and dangers involved.

I'm talking about astral sex. It's not the same as the sex you have when you're corporeal. In some ways it's a lot better, but there are also dangers you need to learn about so you can protect yourself.

Astral sex takes place when you connect your energy to another person or being and allow that energy to flow through the pleasure center of your being. It's not physical, but in some cases you'll derive just as much pleasure from it (or even more!) than if you were having a physical experience.

Find a consenting individual who can go astral when you go astral. Embrace their energy as if you were hugging them, and allow your thoughts to turn to sexual feelings. A warmth and loving positive energy will flow between you two, and it will feel like you are having an energetic orgasm. It's an extremely pleasurable sensation, and as long as you are both into it, you can enjoy this experience and get back to your body feeling quite energized. It's all good.

But there is a darker side to astral sex, and that's when a lower vibrational entity decides it wants to suck energy away from you, and it essentially rapes your energy. Referred to as incubi or succubi, these entities will crawl on top of you while you are still in your body (usually in a sleep paralysis state) and merge their energy with yours. It feels extremely pleasurable, which is why a lot of people don't fight back or pull away.

In fact, sex with a demonic energy or a lower vibrational entity can feel so good that it can become addictive, and the more you allow the entity to drain you, the less resistance you'll have in the future. But you'll wake up from these encounters feeling lethargic and energetically depleted, because the entities are stealing your vital energy from you. It's not healthy. Repeated sex with them can also cause feelings of depression, shame, guilt, and anxiety. It's a downward spiral.

If you want to get them off you, you're going to have to use one of the tools in your arsenal. Calling on the archangels works well, stabbing them with a light sword, or commanding them to leave you alone will work. We'll discuss this more in Chapter 13.

For now, you need to know that merging your sexual energy with a higher vibrational being or a friend is awesome, but that allowing yourself to have sex with lower vibrational beings will drain you badly.

COMMUNICATING WITH THE DEAD

The final interaction I want to discuss is communicating with the dead. When you are in an astral state, you can absolutely interact with and speak with those who have crossed over. There are several ways to accomplish this.

Bring them to you. Go astral and call out to the deceased person you'd like to communicate with. If they are interested in communicating with you, and are paying attention, they may come right to you. You will increase your chances of this being successful if you prepare yourself in advance by thinking about the person or people you want to connect with. You'll be acting like a beacon. Be sure you're in a high vibration when you call them to you. Otherwise, they'll have to lower their frequency considerably in order to communicate with you. Experiment with this and see what happens.

Go to them. You can go astral and move yourself to their energy instead of asking them to come down to your level. This will involve you using your will and intent to get you to the right person. Just as you can focus your intention on meeting up with a friend, you can focus your attention on your deceased loved one and go to them, allowing yourself to be drawn to their energy. Again, be absolutely certain you are in a high vibration (think about the love you have for them) so that you are not inadvertently drawn down to the lower realms where someone may masquerade as your loved one.

Talking to strangers. On some occasions I would be exploring the "afterlife" realms, and I would encounter deceased people I didn't know. I could talk to them, and they would talk to me. Sometimes I would ask their assistance in finding a specific person. They never seemed to know the person I was talking about, which makes sense as there are so many souls out there. But they would often point me to a new level or realm or plane and tell me to try there.

Helping people cross over. One night, early in my astral experiences, I went astral like normal and started flying around my neighborhood. Suddenly I was being pulled at breakneck speed. It was like someone lassoed me and was pulling me with it. I remember soaring through brick buildings and trees, and trying to stop, but I was moving too fast.

When I finally stopped, I was standing in an attic next to a bed. There was a man in the bed and his skin looked burned. He reached out a feeble hand to me and said, "Help me!" I was so scared, I snapped myself back to my body.

But the experience wasn't over. I got pulled out of my body and again felt myself moving through the air at super-fast speed. I landed again at the bedside of this old man. He reached out his hand be-seechingly and said, "Please help me. I don't know what's going on." I took a moment to try to figure out what was happening. He didn't feel evil. In fact, he seemed scared. I looked around his room and saw a brilliant white light. It occurred to me that he was dead and was too afraid to cross over.

I leaned in and touched his hand and said in a reassuring tone, "I think you're dead. You've got to cross over."

He replied, "No, I'm afraid. I just want to stay here in my bed."

I told him not to be afraid to cross over and eventually after some convincing, he agreed to go into the light and was gone.

It was a troubling experience for me because I was very young at the time and had no idea what had just happened. I wasn't expecting to encounter souls who were keeping themselves anchored here after death. It was also troubling because I felt like I didn't have a choice in the matter; I got summoned and couldn't seem to say no.

The next time something like this happened, I went astral and heard a baby crying. I was immediately drawn to the baby as it sounded like it was in distress. I found the baby in a dumpster and realized it had been abandoned and was dying of exposure. I didn't know what to do. It was still alive! I stayed with the baby and comfort-ed its soul until it died and went into the light.

That experience really shook me because, in the next day or two, I read a story in our local paper about a baby who was found dead in a dumpster. I believed it to be the same baby I had sat with. The time and location matched.

After that experience, I realized I didn't need to be afraid of the experience, so I would allow myself to be called by frightened deceased people and I would help reassure them that it was safe to cross over. I actually felt like I was finally doing something useful by being able to astral project. It didn't happen a lot, but it happened enough.

I am not sure this will happen to you. I believe that my strong intuitive abilities and my future work as a medium were probably factors in my even hearing these souls, but try it and see if it's something you're interested in doing. It's altruistic and loving to help a spirit feel safe crossing over.

Part 5
Safe Traveling

CHAPTER 12

Protecting Yourself

You're learning how to travel and perhaps you've even traveled with friends. I hope you're enjoying yourself, and I hope all your experiences have been pleasant, exciting, and fascinating. In the next three chapters, we're going to talk about how to protect yourself while you travel, and what to do if you are challenged by astral baddies. I'm also including a chapter on how to avoid unwanted astral projection because there may come a time when you want to close the door on these experiences, temporarily or for good.

First, we'll talk about how to protect yourself. It's a good habit to adopt whether you expect to encounter an astral nasty or not. I had to learn about protection on the fly because I was the target of so many negative beings that I had to quickly figure out how to protect my body and my astral energy. I had some helpful teachers, both corporeal and non-corporeal, and I am so thankful for their instruction. My goal is to help you set up your protections early so that all, or at least most of your astral experiences are positive.

Astral Shields

First let's talk defense. When you go astral you're going to leave your body behind. After all, there's very little joy in going astral and then standing next to your body the whole night. You might be worried that something will come along and attack your body while you are off touring the cosmos. I'd love to tell you that nothing will bother your body while you're astral, and I hope nothing does, but it can happen, and I want you to be prepared.

Many times when I was astral projecting I'd come back from my travels to find something sniffing around my body, or standing between me and my body, challenging me. It was scary. It was frustrating. It just wasn't cool at all.

I consulted with Sam and I also consulted with my own spirit guides on how to protect my body when I was out of residence. I was told by both of them that I could make a shield of light and place it over my body. They said it would block contact with other beings and keep my body completely safe from harm.

So the next time I left my body I wanted to see if I could make a shield. Sam and the guides had told me I could create a shield using a combination of will, intent, and my own high vibration energy. So the first thing I did was allow intense feelings of love and gratitude to wash over my being. Then I imagined and intended for there to be a white light energy shield around my body. What appeared was a shell, that looked like crystal light, which settled above my body and around the sides.

I reached out to touch the shield and it felt solid. I liked it. I told it to stay put, and off I went for my usual journey. When I came back, my body was as I had left it. I removed the shield when I was ready to get back in my body. It was a simple matter of willing and intending for it to be gone, and gone it went.

Experiment by creating a shield around your body. Your shield may look different than mine. I know some people who just put a strong white light around their body that acts to repel low vibrational beings. I preferred to use something that looked like a hard shell.

Your shield is made of energy and light. Know that nothing harmful can get past it. You will feel a lot safer leaving your body with a shield in place. Even if dark entities are attracted to the light, they won't be able to get in and mess with you.

Now that your body is shielded, let's talk about your astral self. Does it need a shield too? Sometimes when I encountered something scary, I would create a shield of white light around my astral body. But in general, my high vibration was my shield. As long as I was in a high vibration like love, gratitude, compassion, or joy, I didn't encounter low vibrational beings and didn't need to shield myself.

But believe me, there were hundreds of encounters with the dark side, and being able to create an energy shield around my astral body at will became highly necessary. Sometimes I surrounded myself with light, and sometimes I got creative and made a suit of bright light armor. I looked like an astral Valkyrie or Amazon warrior.

The bottom line on shielding is that it may not be necessary, but it's a good habit to get into. Practice making your shields before you need them, and then enjoy your time on the astral plane without fear.

ASTRAL WEAPONS

Now let's talk about offense. You may, upon occasion, encounter a low vibrational being who wants to attack you, steal some of your energy, feed off your fear, or hurt you psychologically. In those cases, a shield is a good start, but it doesn't send the bad guys packing. That's when you want to create something you can use offensively to dispel and disperse their energy.

In my teen years when I was first learning astral projection, I had hundreds of encounters with astral entities that wanted to feed off my energy or hurt me. I learned shielding because of it. But then I talked to Sam about how to proactively get rid of these ookie spookies. He talked to me about creating astral weapons.

You create astral weapons in the same way you create an astral shield; using your will, intent, and vibration. I recall a time when I left my body and flew out my window, intending to go explore the Earth. But something jumped me. I felt a creature pounce on me as soon as I exited my window. He pushed me right down to the ground, and I felt myself beginning to move into the ground. I knew he was trying to push me down to a lower plane. I was frightened and unprepared for the assault.

Once I got my wits about me, I activated my astral shield of light and the being jumped off me. It was like I burned him with the light. But he was still hovering close by. I remember thinking in my mind, "Screw this!" I was tired of being jumped, tired of being the victim, and really tired of playing nice.

I hopped to my astral feet, opened my hand, and willed a sword to appear. I succeeded instantly on my first try. I was holding a long, pointed sword of light and I stabbed the creature with it. It howled and dissipated. Man that felt good! After so many encounters where escape and running back to my body seemed to be my only options, it felt so good to get the upper hand and be able to take action.

Once I dispelled the first creature, I became something of a hunter. I started looking for the low vibrational entities around the neighborhood and would stab them with my sword. It got to be really fun. I felt like an astral warrior, slaying the dark entities for the good of us all. I was eventually able to tune in to people who were being fed on and go there and free them of their entity problems. This got the attention of something really big and really bad, which put me and my friends in a lot of danger. We'll discuss that in the next chapter.

For now, you need to know that you can use your light offensively as well as defensively. I carried a sword when necessary. Instead of a sword, you could use a bow and arrows, a spear, a mace, all made of light. Anything you can think of, you can create. Sometimes I'd dispense with the sword and just shoot light out of my astral hands like a laser. Works just as well. I found that as long as I was aligned with goodness, love, and was working to help others, the light came, and never drained me. I'd get back to my body totally energized.

You will not have to deal with creating astral weapons if you don't want to. At the time that's what I was into, and that's what I did. In my twenties, I spent my time in the higher realms because I wasn't riddled with so much fear, and I retired my light sword.

ASTRAL GUARDIANS

You are not alone on your astral journey. Astral guardians keep the planes in order. Think of them like astral police officers patrolling the realms and keeping the peace. If they didn't, then astral beings would intersect with our plane and run amok, feeding on you while you were at work, on the bus, or sitting at the park. It would be energetic chaos.

However, these guardians can't protect you from your own will and your own actions. If you go poke the beehive, don't be upset when the bees come and sting you. Free will exists on the astral plane. If you consciously engage with an astral entity (good or bad) the guardians will stand back until you cry for help.

So who are these astral guardians?

Archangels. The biggest and baddest of the guardians are the archangels. They keep the doors between our world and the other planes closed. If you have a problem, if you are in trouble, if you fear for your life, you should call upon Archangel Michael. You can call upon other archangels if you desire, but trust me, if you call on Michael, your problems will be solved. Michael and I became good friends back in my teen years because I got myself in hot water many times. He is your fail-safe.

If the archangels are so powerful, how come you are attacked in the first place? Think of it like going into the boxing ring. You are deciding to engage. The archangels respect free will. If you say, "Hey, Michael, I'm going to go play in that astral vampire nest over there. Don't worry about me, I've got my light sword and shield." Then Michael will stand back and let you play, and get hurt if you so choose. But he will always come if you call.

Guardian angels. I tried not to call on Michael unless something was attacking me that I couldn't handle on my own. But along the way I started to notice there were light beings nearby in various states of interaction with me. Sometimes they were right next to me as I traveled, like dolphins who swim near ships. They'd keep their distance, but I'd know they were there. And sometimes I would interact with one or more. When I engaged with them, their energy was so loving and protective. I would sometimes just bask in their light. It was like filling up my gas tank with love and light. Look for them when you're out and about on the astral plane. They can help keep your energy protected and safe and are happy to do so.

Spirit guides. Every time you project, your guides know it and are watching you. Again, free will trumps all, so even if your guides see you in trouble they won't intervene unless you ask them to. Spirit guides are not as powerful as archangels, though. So if you're in real trouble, call the archangels.

Guides should be used as guides. I spent many journeys asking my guides to take me somewhere or show me something. They've been around the block a few times and can show you things you wouldn't even think to ask about. You will feel safe with them.

My guides were also the ones who would help me find and interact with deceased friends and relatives. They've got good connections and are quite useful in the information department. If you don't know your guides and have never interacted with them, you can call to them when you go astral and let them introduce themselves to you. Have a nice chat.

Your friends. Ashley and Jared ended up rescuing me from myself and my encounters often. If you have friends that you travel with or who are accomplished projectors, they can watch your back or help you fight off a horde of angry imps. There were times when I'd hear Ashley calling to me for help, and there were many more times when Sam, Jared, and Ashley heard me calling for help. If they were able, they'd come to my rescue and I to theirs. It pays to make friends with other projectors.

Astral familiars. I mentioned going to Sam's house one night and encountering his astral guardian, which resembled a bull dog. He had put that "dog" there on purpose. When I asked him where he got the animal he said he invited one to be his astral familiar and bound it to himself.

There are creatures on the astral plane that you can ask to guard you. This mutt was one of them. I never had an astral familiar, preferring to use shields and weapons, but if you're so inclined, you could invite an astral familiar to assist and guard you. Just make sure it doesn't turn on you. You've got to have a strong will and be quite confident to manage a familiar. Tread lightly and be wise.

CHOOSING THE CHANNEL

My goal in writing about protection is not to scare you but to prepare you. If you encounter something frightening, you can change the channel. You can move away. You don't have to engage with it.

In the beginning, every time I projected, I felt fear. I would see scary things in my room, waiting for me. At the time, I didn't know about how to change my vibration so that I could move out of phase with those creatures.

Sam told me if I saw the ookie spookies, to just turn my back on them. I thought he was nuts. How can you turn your back on something that's trying to eat you? He said, "Trust me. Just turn your back."

Shortly after I received this sage advice, I projected and saw a huge skeleton sitting in my desk chair. I kid you not. There were prismatic colors swirling around inside him. He stood up and started walking towards me. I was paralyzed with fear. I knew if it touched me, I would die (or so I believed).

But I remembered what Sam said and I flipped around so my back was to the skeleton. There was a palpable shift or click sensation and suddenly I could feel that I was on another plane, a much higher plane. When I looked around the room, I saw only light, not darkness, and the skeleton was gone. I felt a huge sense of relief. I felt free and light! I felt good! No more fear.

After that experience, I knew that my vibration and my plane location was a choice. Yeah, something could pop out and startle you, but you don't have to be afraid of it. Just wave it off, leave its plane. It won't be able to follow you.

If you do get stuck with negative thinking or fear, then you may need to go into fight mode. But trust me, you can step out of the boxing ring anytime you want by switching channels. This is why it's important to master your vibration. Be able to switch to love and gratitude at a moment's notice.

INTENTION, WILL, AND VIBRATION

Your vibration, will, and intention are your greatest allies or your greatest enemies. Whatever thoughts you sow, you shall reap. If you stay in a place of fear, you will attract negative entities to you. If you put yourself in the vibration of love, you will have amazing and positive experiences and encounters.

If you will something into existence, it will be created. So be careful what you create. Likewise, if you need something, you can create it. If you don't believe you can, you can't. Your thoughts manifest quickly on the astral plane. There is no delay.

Control your emotions, your fear, and your desires. Think clearly. Pre-plan for emergencies so you're not in a state of panic. You decide what experiences you're going to have.

And remember that other entities operate under the same conditions. They are using their will and intent against you sometimes. But you can always change the channel and leave them where they are. Try to go into all your experiences from a place of love and gratitude and you will be just fine.

CHAPTER 13

Interactions with Low Vibrational Beings

I sincerely hope that every single one of your astral encounters is positive, and that all your adventures and travels leave you feeling fantastic. It's quite possible that you will never have a bad encounter in your life. But you might, and I want you to know what to do if it happens.

Just like in the waking world, when you travel, it can be so much fun. You get to visit new places, try new things, meet new people. But sometimes when you travel, you get mugged or attacked. It's prudent to know how to protect yourself and avoid the worse areas of town, so you minimize your chances of being attacked, right?

So in this chapter I'll explain who these astral muggers are, why they attack you, and how to recover from an attack if it happens.

FEEDING FRENZY

When you astral project, it's like a light goes on all around you. You light up with a bright white light that says to the rest of the astral denizens, "Hey, look, there's someone over there!" Like moths to a flame, they go to investigate. When they arrive they give you the once over.

Are you easy pickings? Or are you shielded? Are you on their channel, or are you vibrating with love?

If you are in a place of fear and if you don't have any guardians or shields around you, they'll see you as easy prey. These entities love to feed on fear, so if you go astral and are afraid, they will start attacking your energy in an attempt to drain you dry. You become like dog food to them. It's not even so much that they want to hurt you. You're simply food to them, and they're hungry.

If you go astral and immediately put yourself in a place of love, gratitude, compassion, joy, and confidence, they will still see your light, but be unable to reach you. It's like a mugger trying to reach you while you are inside a shop surrounded by police. They're not going to be able to touch you, feed off you, or attack you. Your best defense against these bad guys is to simply not walk in their neighborhoods when you're astral. Don't be where they are, and they are always on Fear Street.

ASTRAL ENTITIES

So what exactly could you encounter while on the astral plane? Let's go over the most common entities you'll find on the fear channel and discuss their power level and ability to do you serious harm. This list is by no means exhaustive, but it will give you a good idea of what you might expect and how to handle it.

Imps. Think of these guys like mosquitoes. They swarm you almost as soon as you go astral, biting and sucking at your energy. They are not very powerful, and you can swat them away with your energy as long as you don't succumb to fear. One good blast of light and love and they will recoil and go away. They're going to appear small and dark, no bigger than a small bat. They're not going to be your worst problem.

Poltergeists. These are like a higher level version of imps. They are stronger, bigger, and more mischievous than imps. They will play around with your mind and your reality in order to create a vibration of fear inside you. Think of them like tenderizers and you're the meat.

They'll scare the proverbial pants off you so that you make a tastier snack. Again, just change the channel, cast some love into the room, or tell them to take a hike.

Incubi and succubi. An incubus or a succubus is a sexual creature who will climb on top of you in bed or push you to the ground and attempt to rape you. They will create sexual feelings inside you and then feed off that energy. At first, it can seem like a very pleasurable experience, even bringing you to a full orgasm, but they will leave you feeling so worn out and depleted with all your energy sapped from your body. There are better and easier ways to get your sexual needs met.

An incubus is a masculine entity and a succubus is feminine. You'll know what you've got by the body parts you feel touching you. People often experience them during sleep paralysis. The less you're able to fight back, the easier it is for them.

If you're in sleep paralysis when you're attacked, call upon Archangel Michael to assist you in removing them. If you're already astral, they are less likely to attack you because you won't be easy prey, but if it should happen, just put up a shield and run them through with your light sword.

Alternatively, you can shoot love and light at them. They don't care for that. Resist the urge to engage with them in sexual play, even if it feels good. The same way a bed bug will anesthetize your skin before it sinks its teeth into you, a succubus or incubus will put you in a state of physical pleasure in order to lull you into letting them suck away your energy. If you let them do it once, they'll come back for more, and you can slip into such a low state physically that you become depressed or sick.

Astral vampires. I'm not sure what they call themselves, but I call them astral vampires because that's how they look. Humanoid but not human. In between animal and human I would say. Small beady red eyes, fangs, funky looking pointy ears, and claws at the end of their fingers. They're conscious, intelligent, and powerful. They're not remotely nice.

This is the story of my encounter with an astral vampire, which I alluded to in an earlier chapter. My boyfriend and I were having an argument in the middle of the day. I was sitting on my floor, and he was sitting on my bed. The fight petered out, and before I knew it, we had both fallen asleep. That was odd and unusual for me to just fall asleep on the floor.

When I woke up, it was dark and the clock read midnight. I felt something wrong in the air. I decided to go downstairs and investigate. I felt like something was watching me, and when I went through my dining room I thought I saw a red orb bobbling around outside the window. The air had a strange crackling energy to it. I felt fear and raced back upstairs.

Instead of waking my boyfriend who was asleep on the bed, I decided to go astral and see what this energy was. If I was sensing it on the physical plane, I could only imagine how powerful it was on the astral.

I went astral and manifested my light sword. I flew downstairs and looked out the dining room window again. This time instead of a red orb, I saw two red eyes staring at me. I flooded my dining room with intense white light to keep this thing out. I figured my job was done.

I flew back upstairs intending to get back into my body, mission accomplished. But there he was, an astral vampire standing between me and my body. In a sibilant whisper he said, "Are you sure you want to go back to your body?"

I replied, "Yes, God damn you!" and he recoiled like I had flung holy water on him. He dissipated.

But that's not the end of the story. I climbed into my body but couldn't merge. Weird. So I got up, still in astral form, and went to my boyfriend's body. I saw his astral self and my intention was to get him to wake me up. But as I got close to him, his astral hands snaked around my astral neck and he started choking me. I pried his hands off me and reassured him it was just me, then begged him to wake up so he could wake me up. I knew that if he just shook my body a little, it would cause my astral body to snap back into my physical body.

He assured me he would wake up, but he didn't. He just went back to sleep. So frustrating! Eventually, I got back in my body and got myself up, now fully corporeal. I went to wake up my boyfriend on the bed, but as I gently shook him, his hands snaked out and grabbed me around my neck and he flung me onto the bed and started choking me.

It seemed like he was still asleep. I pummeled at him until he woke up fully. He let go of me, and before I could say anything he said, "I just had the weirdest dream. There was a vampire in the room, and when he got close to me I choked him and threw him out the window."

I said, "That wasn't a dream. That happened, on the astral plane." We talked about it for a while. We were both really shaken by the encounter.

I was annoyed by the astral creature and decided if I ever encountered him again I would be ready. When that day finally came, I went astral and saw him beckoning to me outside my window. He had strong mind-control powers, and I could feel him eroding my will. It was like I was under a spell. But I wasn't. I retained my full awareness and resisted his urgings.

I flew out the window at full speed and tackled him. Then I pushed him down to the ground, sat on top of him, whipped up my light sword, and stabbed him through the chest. He turned into black smoke and sunk into the ground.

I never saw him again. He had so many qualities of mythical vampires that I started to wonder if perhaps the story was based on the author's own encounter with such a creature on the astral plane. Regardless, I was very happy to never encounter one again.

If you encounter an astral vampire, take heed, they are somewhat powerful. I'm not sure what he would have done to me if he had gotten a hold of me, but I'm glad I never found out. Run them through with your sword. You can try moving to a different channel. I never got that opportunity. As the years progressed, I kept my vibration high every time I traveled, that might explain why I never encountered one again.

Shadow people. A lot of people report shadow people when they are awake. It's like you see someone move past you but when you turn to look head on, you see nothing. They flit and fly by too quickly to really see them.

Well imagine looking at them while on the astral plane. You can see them a lot more clearly. I don't have a lot of experience with shadow people, but some of my friends do. They report that shadow people appear human on the astral plane, but are definitely not living beings with bodies to go back to. They roam around the astral plane. Perhaps they are lost souls who chose not to cross over. They too feed off your fear, it's probably what keeps them at the frequency needed to avoid crossing over. I also get the feeling they weren't exactly up-standing citizens while alive. Avoid them if you can. Remember to just change the channel.

Demons. Well, let's just get right up into it. Demons exist. However, be-fore you whip out the crucifix and start praying, please understand that the likelihood of you ever encountering a demon is really, really small.

Demons are totally kick ass, bad ass, conscious, intelligent, dark energies that want nothing more than to hurt you, kill you, or possess you. These are not religious demons from Hell or the ones you see in the movies. Think of them as the antithesis to angels. Instead of love and light, they are fear and control. They are strong and powerful, and there's not a lot that stops them. As such, the archangels keep a very tight leash on these guys.

That does NOT mean that you should stand in the center of your bedroom while astral and say, "Demons, come and get me!" because if you invite one to you, it will come. Once it gets there, it will grab hold of you like a dog with a bone, and thrash and beat you into a pulp. Even when you cry out for mercy, and mercy shows up, you will be wrecked emotionally and physically for days, months or possibly even years if you have a mental breakdown.

It's like when you go to the zoo. They don't let you play with the li-ons, right? Only the trained professionals can interact with the lions. If you crawl into the lions' exhibit, don't be surprised if it tears off your limbs. But you're the one who decides if you're going to do that. No one will ever push you into a demon's den. Don't go looking for trou-ble or you will find it.

Ashley, Jared, and I ran into some trouble with a demonic entity, and it took us four months and a lot of assistance before we could get it away from us. It took a strong toll on us all, though. Jared had a psy-chotic episode and became very violent. Ashley became suicidal, but she got help and recovered. And I developed an anxiety disorder that I eventually got over, as well. But it took years to fully recover.

Demons don't just suck your energy away. They pull you apart and put you back together wrong. It takes serious sorting out to survive and recover from a demonic attack.

If you think you're being attacked or targeted by a demon, stop projecting until you no longer feel the demonic energy around you. Demon energy can pervade your waking life. Luckily nothing too terrible happened to me or any of my friends, but we were scarred for years after our encounter. That encounter was one of the reasons I tried to shut down all my intuitive abilities in my twenties.

If you've got a demon on your tail, seek professional help from a demonologist (google them), or someone experienced in demon detachment like an angel therapy practitioner, a priest trained in how to deal with demons, or a paranormal investigation team with experience in these matters.

Remember this above all…love trumps fear. Don't go to the demon zoo and you won't end up as a demon's chew toy. Use common sense and avoid the dark if you can help it. Vibrate with love and light, and you will be just fine!

NEGATIVE ENTITY ATTACHMENTS

In my work as a professional intuitive, psychic, and medium, I occasionally encounter clients who have a negative entity attachment. This is a serious but totally fixable situation. It's also extremely rare. In several thousand readings, I've only encountered it six times.

A negative entity attachment (NEA for short) occurs when a low vibration entity from the astral plane decides it wants to attach to your energy and not let go. So instead of it just feeding off you while you sleep or go astral, it's feeding off you all the time. It's with you all the time. It tethers its energy to you and goes where you go, using your energy as a snack whenever it gets hungry.

An NEA will also begin to influence you. It will get into your mind and give you ideas that aren't very healthy. Maybe you'll feel like you want to start doing heavy drugs. Maybe you'll become violent or angry around people you used to love. Maybe you'll begin to have thoughts of suicide. You may become depressed, lethargic, paranoid. You can become physical ill or develop chronic health conditions.

How do you know if you've got an attachment or you're just having a bad time in life?

You'll go from having a normal, healthy, routine life, to suddenly and without cause doing drugs, becoming promiscuous, sabotaging your career, losing your energy, becoming suicidal. In other words, your friends will be thinking, "What the heck just happened to Larry? It's like he's a different person now. He just turned on a dime." There won't be any real world triggers causing this, just a sudden or noticeable change in your personality and habits.

NEAs are particularly attracted to people who are depressed, sad, angry, fearful, or in other low vibrational states. This is why I don't recommend even attempting astral projection unless you are in a healthy and positive state of mind. Otherwise, it's like handling black mold without gloves on.

Like I said, the chances of you attracting an NEA are slim to none. For them to stay attached to you, you've got to have no positive energy at all. Which brings me to how to get rid of them. They don't like it when you've got your stuff together. They don't like love, joy, gratitude, or compassion. They can't hold on to that energy. So if you've got a verified NEA, you're going to have to get help or work on improving your vibration on your own. It can be difficult to do this without help because the NEA will try to prevent you from reaching a high vibration. So it's helpful to get some therapy or work with a psychic or energy healer who can get the NEA off you long enough for you to heal.

Worst case scenario, Archangel Michael can assist you as well. Call to him when you're in trouble and let him do the heavy lifting. But if you don't fix your energy afterwards, you'll just invite the NEA back.

LOSING AND RESTORING YOUR ENERGY

I often went to high school totally drained and depleted from a night of fighting astral bad guys. It's got to be how boxers feel after a match. Partly it was my fault for seeking them out because I really enjoyed sending them packing, and partly it was because I'd attracted the attention of the astral mob whose boss wanted me gone. I have only myself to blame. If you open a can of worms, you're going to get worms!

Your vital energy is stored in your astral body. It's your soul, your spirit, your consciousness. If some of the energy is left behind, or sucked away, you're going to feel like a toy with a dying battery inside of you.

So let's discuss ways to restore your energy if you've lost it, and these tips will also include prevention.

Keep yourself in good physical health. Don't let your body deteriorate. Feed it lots of water, good healthy foods, and exercise it. You need to live in this body. It has a vibration too. Don't let it become slothful, overweight, or dehydrated if you can help it. Coming back from an astral journey to a whole body will keep a lot of energy inside your body.

Don't project every day. There came a time when I was projecting every night. It was too easy and too fun, so I did it a lot. But if I was sorely depleted or I'd lost a few fights, I would take some time to fully ground myself back in the physical world, and let my batteries recharge. There's no point in projecting if you're already on empty. That's like deciding to go on a road trip with a quarter tank of gas.

Don't leave your body when you're sick. Try not to project when you've got a fever or other illness. It leaves the body weaker and less able to defend against physical threats like viruses and bacteria. If you do leave your body while sick, go seek healing on the higher planes. There are many beings there that can restore some of your energy. Let your angels protect and guide you while you journey.

Be of good cheer. Vibration determines your experience. Walk around your life happy and of good cheer. Raise other people's vibrations around you. Be loving, kind, considerate, and caring of your fellow man. Laugh. Sing. Dance. Make other people feel better. Nothing will restore your energy like someone blessing you or gifting you with gratitude. Help others and you'll help yourself. Then when you project, you'll be riding such a high vibration that you could easily come back with more energy instead of less.

Get some good rest. When you're astral projecting, you are not sleeping. Your mind and body aren't going through the same rhythms as they do when you're just plain sleeping and dreaming. Take some time to nap or rest on days when you feel energetically or physically drained.

Only interact with good beings. If you do often find yourself depleted of energy, make a point to only interact with the positive beings on the astral plane. Go to the higher realms. Talk to a deceased loved one, an angel, or guide. You will return to your body with tons of energy. It's like going shopping in the energy grocery store.

BODY SNATCHING

One of the top ten questions people ask me about astral projection is whether something else could take their body while they are out. No. Remember, your astral cord is your bookmark. Nothing can slip in while you're out.

At worst, something might feed on you, suck on your energy, or try to drain you like you were a battery, but nothing is going to take over your body, leaving you hovering outside of it, knocking to get back in.

I never projected and came back to my body to find something trying to slip into it or take it over. I encountered beings that were picking at it, or trying to scare me away from it, but nothing that ever tried to slip into it.

Hollywood movies have put this fear into many would-be projectors, which is unfortunate. If you're afraid something will take over your body, you'll project right into fear central and have a bad trip. Don't succumb to this line of thinking. Body snatching is not real.

ASTRAL PROJECTION IS FUN...REALLY!

My intention is not to frighten you, but to prepare you. You can use astral projection to have the adventure and experiences of a lifetime. Or you can dig around in the muck and play with demons. It's totally your choice. If you decide to go spelunking in the dark, just make sure you bring your light with you.

CHAPTER 14

Avoiding Astral Projection

In this book, I've taught you how to astral project safely and effective-ly. But at least a quarter of the questions I get about astral projection are from people desperately trying to stop or avoid projecting in the first place. They are having encounters that frighten them so badly that they just want it to stop.

When you constantly wake in a state of sleep paralysis, or if you are being attacked by entities and you don't want to learn to fight or raise your vibration, then you can stop or prevent astral projection from occurring.

If you are plagued by unwanted astral encounters, this chapter is for you. I'll explain how to prevent astral projection, but bear in mind, there isn't one single switch you can flip and turn it off. Just as it takes some time, energy, attention, and practice to learn astral projection, it will take some effort to avoid it if you're having unwanted experiences. So do the best you can.

Positions that Hinder Projection

Remember how I explained that lying on your back is the best position from which to project? Well, if you want to avoid astral projection, you'll want to avoid ever sleeping or napping on your back. Instead, try sleeping on your side or on your stomach. You are much less likely to experience sleep paralysis in these positions.

Also, sleep with your limbs crossed. If you cross your ankles or hands you will be more anchored in your body. Imagine if you were in a boat in turbulent waters and you were afraid of capsizing or being tossed out of your boat. You could wrap your feet and hands in rope and stay anchored in the boat even if the elements try to toss you out. Crossing your limbs will hinder your projection.

Try Snuggling

It's almost impossible to project when you're touching someone else's energy. If you can find a partner to snuggle at night, you will have less encounters with unwanted astral projection and sleep paralysis.

Touching another person disrupts your energy. Just as having someone shake you awake can cause you to snap back into your body, touching someone else physically will create a disruptive pattern from the get go. Your incidences of spontaneous astral projection and sleep paralysis will go down significantly.

If you don't have a snuggle-partner, but you have a pet, see if you can get your animal companion to sleep next to you on your bed.

Stay Grounded

Just as you had to prepare yourself energetically to be able to astral project, one of the best ways to avoid astral projection is to turn your attention and energy back to the physical world.

Stay grounded. When you go to sleep at night think about your daily life and your to-do list. Think about what you're going to do the next day, think about any problems you may have, or any issues you're trying to work out. Anything that keeps your mind on your life will help you avoid astral projection.

Also, be physical. Do some exercise before you go to sleep. Concentrate some of your time and energy on building up your muscles, stamina, endurance, strength, etc. People who are very physically oriented tend to project less often than the airy fairy spiritual woo-woo types who listen to spirits all day. If you're not tuned in to the ether channel, the ether channel won't tune in to you.

CLOSE THE DOOR

Just as immersing yourself in the study of astral projection is a good way to bring on an encounter, if you want to avoid astral encounters you have to close that door.

Stop pursuing psychic abilities. If you're studying intuition and trying to improve your intuition, you're holding that door open. Stop tuning in to your own spirit guides and intuition, at least until you've got a handle on your projections.

Create a permanent shield. Set up a shield around your body and then forget it. This isn't the kind of shield you put up when you begin an astral journey. This is the kind of shield you put up that says, "Closed. Out of business. Sorry." You're basically turning off your light. This will help you avoid attracting negative entities whose presence might induce a sleep paralysis episode in order to feed off your energy.

Close your crown chakra. Your crown chakra is located at the top of your head. A bright white light comes out of your crown chakra and connects you with Source energy. It is the doorway from which you project. Close it.

Imagine a manhole cover in place on your crown. Bolt it down so nothing can pry it open. Again you're telling the world you are closed. Don't be surprised though if you feel less connected spiritually.

Close your brow chakra. Your brow chakra is located right between your eyebrows and is responsible for your intuitive connection to the unseen world. Close that sucker down too. It's like closing your eyes so you can't see anymore.

Just imagine putting a cap on it like you'd see on a water bottle. Screw the cap onto your chakra and tell the astral world, "I can't see you because I'm not looking at you anymore."

Close any open doors. If you've been astral projecting and are now deciding you want to stop, make sure to close any astral doors you may have left open. You can do this by pulling your energy back to you. Any energy you've left tethered to friends, locations, any book-marked frequencies you've generated, you want to recall all that energy, suck it back into your body, and zip yourself closed. You can do all of this via meditation without having to go astral to do it.

JUST SAY NO

Quit cold turkey. Stop astral projecting. If you want it to stop, you can't keep your toes in the water. When you awaken in sleep paralysis mode, resist the urge to slip out of your body, even if you feel the tingling sensation or hear the high-pitched whine. If you do find yourself moving out of your body, pull yourself back in as fast as possible.

Shout NO into the void. If you find yourself opening up, you just close right back down. Pull your energy back inside you and resist the urge to expand. If something tugs at you, beckons to you, or tries to assist you, you tell it NO.

If you normally project with friends, make sure you tell them you're done and not to come pick you up. Just having an astral person next to you could trigger a projection, especially if you used to travel with them frequently. Just like when you're trying to give up drinking you don't hang out with friends at a bar, let your friends know you are serious and not to tempt you.

Stop studying astral projection, stop talking about it, stop reading about it. Stop praying, stop meditating, stop raising your vibration. You need to broadcast the "I'm done" message.

AVOID NAPPING AND LUCID DREAMING

Oh, those pesky but refreshing naps. If you want to avoid astral projection, try to avoid napping. If you must nap, sleep on your side or stomach. Sleep paralysis is more likely to happen during naps, and you want to avoid sleep paralysis at all costs, or the astral door will remain open.

If you are an accomplished lucid dreamer, you're just asking for trouble. Staying conscious while sleeping is a good way to slip into an unwanted projection. To avoid lucid dreaming, think about your problems before you go to sleep. Your subconscious mind will take over and use your dream time to process your problems and issues and help you work out a solution.

KEEP THE LIGHTS ON

If nothing else works, try sleeping with your lights on for a while. It's a great way to keep the astral bad guys at bay. It's not a permanent solution, but if you're wanting to avoid astral projection because you're being attacked or stalked by something negative, then keeping the lights on will disrupt the dark frequencies around you. This will give you time to heal, restore your energy, and possibly avoid a nervous breakdown if you're about to have one.

LAST RESORT

As a last resort, if you want to avoid astral projection from the get go, or you need to take a serious break, just ask Archangel Michael to assist you. Tell him to keep your door closed, keep the negative entities at bay, and even keep your guides or other helpful beings from enticing you out. Think of him like a bodyguard. He will keep you zipped up and away from the astral plane.

Your Astral Projection Checklist

Read through the book thoroughly before you begin your journey, then use this checklist to help you remember the steps to learning and mastering astral projection, and knowing what to expect once you get out there.

Preparation

Select a location: Decide if you will use a bed, couch, or recliner.

Keep a log book: Use a log book to track your progress and get an idea of when and how you are most successful. Then use that information to plan your projections better.

Control the noise: Turn off your alarms, put the dog out, keep the doors closed.

Clear your mind: Practice turning off your thoughts through meditation and solving your worldly problems as much as possible.

Meditate: Learn how to control your breathing, learn to relax, learn to control your thoughts and your consciousness.

Immerse yourself: Read, sleep, and think about astral projection as much as possible.

Get social support: Find people online and in person who can help you or who are willing to discuss it with you openly.

Pick a sleep position: Learn to sleep on your back with your limbs uncrossed for greatest success.

Pick a time of day: Decide if you prefer to project in the daytime, at the beginning of your night, in the middle, or at the end of your night. Different times will offer a different level of success. Experiment to find the one that works best for you.

Learn to lucid dream: Nothing will increase your success as much as mastering lucid dreaming. Learn to keep your mind conscious while your body is asleep and you will carry this mastery into your astral projection experiences.

Master your consciousness: While you are awake notice consciously that you are awake. It's a good habit to get into and will help you astral project.

ACHIEVING SEPARATION

Know the indicative sensations:
- Sleep paralysis: You are awake but can't move or open your eyes.
- Dual vision: You can see but your physical eyes are closed.
- Hypnagogic hallucinations: You see and hear beings around you and unusual sounds.
- Tingling: You feel intense tingling inside your body.
- High-pitched whine: You hear a high-pitched whine that sounds like acceleration or a jet plane taking off down the runway.

Overcome your fear: The more prepared you are for what awaits you, the less fearful you're going to be. Have a plan ready to go.

Control your excitement: Getting too excited when you achieve separation can pull you back into your body, so learn to be nonchalant about your success so you can stay out longer.

Move out of your body:

- Stretch out: Lift your arms into the air and let your body follow them up.
- Roll out: Roll off your bed and to the side.
- Teleport out: Pop yourself out of your body to a new location away from your body.
- Sink down: Release your body and let your astral self sink down out of your back.
- Get assistance: Ask your guides or friends to assist you.
- Avoid drugs: A drug-induced projection may or may not be real, plus you can get trapped someplace you don't want to be, with someone you don't want to be stuck with.

NAVIGATE THE ASTRAL REALMS

Travel options:

- Move through space: Roam your neighborhood, visit friends and family.
- Move through time: Visit the past or the future.
- Move through objects: Learn to push your way through solid objects like they're not even there, because they aren't.
- Practice speeding up: Floating and walking will only get you so far, practice flying at super speeds.

Where to go once you're out:

- Prime material plane: This is the earthly three-dimensional plane you're in right now.
- The lower planes: This is where the low vibrational beings hang out. Avoid.
- The higher realms: Where you can interact with celestial beings, spirit guides, angels, deceased loved ones, and a host of other lovely folk.
- The astral highway: Like a freeway system that connects all the planes together. Spend short amounts of time standing on the highway or you will get run over.

- Galaxies, planets, and space: The sky isn't the limit! Go beyond the Earth and out into space. Don't worry about distance. You can go anywhere.

Interacting with others:
- Make a visit: Visit people you know and people you don't know. Be respectful!
- Travel with friends: Get some other projectors with you and travel together. You'll need to really plan this out well in order to be on the same frequency at the same time.
- Astral sex: Share some astral ecstasy with some willing friends.
- Communicate with the dead: Go to them or ask them to come to you but be ready for the experience. You can also assist people in transitioning to the other side.

SAFE TRAVELING

Protect yourself:
- Learn to shield your astral and physical bodies.
- Learn to create astral weapons if you need to go on offense.
- Connect with the astral guardians who will save you when you're in trouble.
- Connect with your spirit guides who can keep you from sinking into the lower realms.
- Master your intention and will, since they are what determine your experiences.
- Learn to change the channel. If you don't like where you are, you can move to a different frequency.

Avoid astral entities:
Things you may encounter but probably want to avoid include: imps, succubi, incubi, astral vampires, poltergeists, shadow people, demons. Learn what they are and how to defeat them.

Negative entity attachments are possible but not likely. Stay in a place of love and gratitude and you will easily avoid having something negative attach itself to you.

Learn how to restore your energy so you are not drained by your experiences or encounters.

Remember that body snatching is not possible. Nothing is going to take up residence in your body while you're out. Keep your protections in place to guard your energy, though.

Avoiding Astral Projection:

If you need to take a break or you need to stop astral projecting altogether, follow these steps:

- Sleep on your side or stomach.
- Snuggle another person, stay touching all night.
- Stay grounded in the physical world, stop thinking about, reading about, or discussing astral projection.
- Close any doors you may have opened. Cut any energetic threads that tie you to the astral plane.
- Shut down your intuitive capabilities, and don't open your chakras.
- Avoid napping, but if you do nap, sleep on your side with your limbs crossed if you can.
- Avoid lucid dreaming as it can easily lead to a projection experience.
- Sleep with the lights on until you've gotten away from anything hunting you.

Enjoy the Journey

I want to end this book by making a wish. It is my hope that you use the techniques and strategies in this book to experience the joy and magic that is astral projection. I hope you will have many positive encounters, travel to amazing places, communicate with high-vibration beings, and even get some friends to travel with you.

Astral projection is a skill you can master and keep with you for a lifetime. When you realize that you are a soul inside a body, and that your soul can never be lost, you will enjoy your life more and no longer fear death.

People who astral project understand that although our physical existence has an expiration date, our souls can never die. When you awaken your consciousness you will shine like a beacon into the cosmos. You will begin to remember who you really are and why you incarnated.

My wish is that astral projection will enrich your life as it has mine. I wish you many pleasant journeys out of your body and encounters that excite and thrill you. Carry love and peace in your heart. Good luck on your journey!

ABOUT THE AUTHOR

Erin Pavlina discovered and developed her intuition at a very early age. Today, her skill as a psychic medium combined with her witty sense of humor and compassionate, down-to-earth personality makes her one of the most sought-after intuitive counselors in the world.

Erin has written hundreds of articles related to personal, spiritual, and psychic development, which you can find on her popular blog. She also answers reader questions via YouTube videos, teleseminars, and podcasts.

Erin lives in Las Vegas, NV with her two children. In her free time, she assists law enforcement agencies with her intuitive abilities, and volunteers on a search and rescue team. For more information on Erin, her books, products, and classes, or to book a session with her, visit her website at ErinPavlina.com.